Twayne's English Authors Series

Sylvia E. Bowman, *Editor*

INDIANA UNIVERSITY

John Braine

 62

John Braine

By JAMES W. LEE

North Texas State University

Twayne Publishers, Inc.   ::   New York

For
CARL BENSON
and
W. R. PATRICK

Preface

THE purpose of this book is to introduce readers to John Braine's novels and to explain something of the times and forces which have shaped them. In this study of Braine's writing, chapters devoted to each of his four novels discuss plot, theme, characterization, setting, style, and various other aspects of fiction. Though the criticism represents no specific school, a great deal of close textual analysis is made in an attempt to see the whole of each novel. One short chapter presents a survey and analysis of the six sketches that Braine published in *The New Statesman,* and another sets forth a conclusion which attempts to draw together the various threads that run throughout this study, as well as make some summary statements about Braine's work. Part of Chapter 1 is an attempt to survey the British novel of the 1950's and early 1960's as it pertains to Braine's development as a writer.

I should like to thank Dean Robert Toulouse and the Faculty Research Council of North Texas State University for a grant which provided me with research assistance and time off to complete this book. Professors E. Garrett Ballard and E. S. Clifton aided in numerous ways, especially in arranging a compatible schedule for me.

Two very competent research assistants—Miss Mary Alice Conklin and Miss Carol Vaughan—typed the first drafts from my illegible handwriting and aided me with many suggestions. Professors Hugh Kirkpatrick and Giles Mitchell read the manuscript and made useful suggestions. I should also like to thank Miss Sylvia E. Bowman, editor of Twayne's English Authors Series, and Miss Vinita Davis of the North Texas State University library.

My greatest debts are to Carroll Rich who read and criticized the entire manuscript, to Gena Poore who read the proofs, and to my wife Florence Lee who typed the final copy and who has been "As one, in suffering all, that suffers nothing."

JAMES W. LEE

Denton, Texas

Contents

Contents

Chronology

1922   John Braine, son of Fred and Katherine Braine, born April 13, in Bradford, Yorkshire.

1933–   Attended St. Bede's Grammar School in Bradford; left
1938   without taking certificate, but was graduated by correspondence four years later.

1938–   Worked in bookshop, furniture store, pharmaceutical
1940   laboratory, and piston-ring factory.

1940   Became assistant in Bingley Public Library, Yorkshire.

1940–   Served as telegrapher in Royal Navy; invalided out with
1943   tuberculosis.

1943–   Resumed position as assistant, Bingley Public Library, be-
1951   coming chief assistant in 1949.

1951–   Free-lance writer in London.
1952

1950–   Published six short sketches in *The New Statesman*.
1957

1952–   In hospital at Grassington with tuberculosis.
1954

1954–   Branch Librarian, Northumberland County Library.
1956

1955   Married Helen Patricia Wood.

1956–   Branch Librarian, West Riding of Yorkshire County Li-
1957   brary.

1957   *Room at the Top.*

1959   *The Vodi (From the Hand of the Hunter).*

1962   *Life at the Top.*

1964   *The Jealous God.* Lecture tour of United States.

CHAPTER 1

Introduction

WHEN John Braine's first novel, *Room at the Top*, was published in 1957, it became an instant success: its sales were large, *The Daily Express* serialized it, and a film was made of it the following year. What the novel had not done toward making Braine's name known internationally, the motion picture did. The movie, starring Laurence Harvey and Simone Signoret, was widely acclaimed as one of the best pictures of 1958, and a number of awards were given to it. In a few months' time, John Braine became a celebrity in both literary and cinematic circles. Some critics thought him to have the great talent that might save the British novel from a growing effeteness.

The center of this publicity, John Gerard Braine, was born in the city of Bradford on April 13, 1922. His parents, Fred and Katherine Braine, were lower-middle-class Catholics; his mother was a librarian whose Irish-Catholic family came, along with a colony of Irish, to Yorkshire during the potato famine of the 1840's. John Braine wrote—and continues to write—in several traditions; but none is stronger than the Yorkshire provincialism that directly colors all his work. He is a Yorkshireman both by birth and by inclination, as stated on the dust jacket of one of his novels. Strongly presented in all his novels is the quality of life in urban, industrialized Bradford, as well as life in the still rural areas of the West Riding.

I *Bradford*

The West Riding of Yorkshire is one of the most isolated sections in the British Isles. David Storey, one of Braine's younger Yorkshire contemporaries, says that—unlike other isolated areas of Britain—the West Riding is almost completely cut off from outside influences. It is landlocked, having no great seaport; it is cut off from the north and west by "bare uplands"; from the south by "vast, featureless plains"; and from the east by the North Sea. The West Riding is a prosperous area of three mil-

13

lion people who are "largely crammed together in two deep and narrow valleys on the eastern slope of the Pennines, with a complex social and political history." [1]

Storey, who calls the area introverted and "obsessively puritan," considers its ingrown personality to be a result of its industrialism and its emphasis on practicality. The individual man is absorbed into a society in which the rich and poor are more alike than different: "It is the area of the practical ascetic, the man who fights his battles ... in the market place, the stock exchange, or on the factory floor. It has, appropriately, a very simple morality: that work is good, and that indolence is, not so much deplorable or unfortunate, as evil." [2] In Storey's own mining community, things were even simpler—physical work was good; mental work, evil. [3] In such an area, an artist is not accepted; in fact, he is barely tolerated. Though it is the area of the Brontës, there is little history of a literary life ever having flourished there. Braine, Keith Waterhouse, and David Storey all represent a new movement in Yorkshire life; for each is engaged in explaining the region to the rest of the world and to itself.

John Braine's writings reflect much of the general nature of the area. He uses the speech, the landscape, and the people of his home county in all his works. This provincialism is consciously done, for he is attempting to portray the microcosmic life of the region. But, more subtly and on an unconscious level, the influence of the North is stamped on his writings. His style reflects the plainness and spareness of Yorkshire life; and his morality—the dedication to work, to duty, and to living ascetically—is akin to the ethics that David Storey mentioned in his comments about the life of the region. Both *Room at the Top* and *Life at the Top* excoriate the "soft" life and the abandonment of work, duty, and discipline.

As important to Braine's work as the generalized region is the town of Bradford, which has long been considered by Englishmen as a kind of archetypal industrial city. The town's importance as a center of the wool trade goes back many centuries; in fact, it is thought that spinning and weaving were first done there as early as the twelfth century. T. S. Eliot's mentioning of Bradford in *The Waste Land* is not the first attack upon the commercial ethos of that city. It was to the city of Bradford that John Ruskin went to dedicate a new exchange building, but dedicated himself instead to attacking the whole basis of local and national architecture. In this speech, found in *The Crown of Wild Olive,* he says that a people get the kind of buildings that reflect their spirit; and, needless to say, he felt that the spirit of the Bradfordians was bleared and seared with trade.

In an interview with J. B. Priestley published in 1958,[4] Braine indicates his own feelings about the nature of life in Bradford when he calls his home town one "which more than any other in England is dominated by a success ethos," a city dedicated almost completely to making money out of the wool trade. While Bradford, Braine admits, is not a city of "illiterate boors," it possesses no "leisured and cultivated middle class." [5] The city, the shire, and even the whole of the industrial North are seen in Braine's novels much as they are pictured in his interview with Priestley. Towns like Warley and Dufton—names that Braine uses for Bradford in his novels—are drab, soot-covered places where human life is secondary to trade. Little culture is evident: the very rich are like Abe Brown in *Room* and *Life at the Top,* and the poorer classes are similar to Dick Corvey in *The Vodi,* Braine's second novel. No one in the novels escapes the deadness of a trade-ridden society. The actuality of Bradford life shows through clearly and intentionally in the novels.

II *Irish-Catholic Background*

Another influence on John Braine's life that figures in his writings is the Irish-Catholic background of his family. Even as late as Braine's boyhood in the early 1930's, being an Irishman in the British North put one in a distinguishable minority. In the reminiscent sketch "Irish Quarter" in *The New Statesman,* Braine writes of the ghetto-like Irish section of Bradford; for being both Irish and Catholic sets one significantly apart in the puritan, nonconformist North. Furthermore, if one descended from a people that had come as laborers eighty or ninety years before, he was stamped rather strongly as working class, or at best as lower middle class. Only in a couple of the sketches and in the fourth novel, *The Jealous God,* is the Irish-Catholic life detailed; however, the lower-middle-class background is evident in all the novels. Braine's three major characters—Joe Lampton, Dick Corvey, and Vincent Dungarvan—are all men from the lower orders of society, and all of them are concerned about their status. Of the three factors in Braine's early life—region, class, and church—it is hard to choose one as the most significant influence on his novels, for all figure prominently.

Braine attended the Thackley Board School—a state-run lower
school—until he was eleven; then he entered St. Bede's Grammar School in Heaton, a Bradford suburb. There he remained
until he was sixteen. The Protestant atmosphere of the state
school was replaced by the strict Catholicism of St. Bede's, which
was run by clergymen. The Protestantism of the board school
was not oppressive, Braine says in a *Spectator* essay;[6] but one
was always aware that, as a Catholic, he was somewhat different
from the rest of the students. The villains of the history classes
at Thackley, for instance, were Philip of Spain and Queen Mary,
both Catholic monarchs. Braine's great fear during his board-
school days was that, if he did poorly on his examinations, he
might fail to get into St. Bede's and have to go instead to
Thorpe Academy, which he called the Blacking Factory or
"Thorpe Academy for Thickheads." [7] Fortunately, he passed his
examinations and was admitted to St. Bede's, which he attended
between 1933 and 1938. He left without taking a certificate; and,
as is the case with a number of young writers of the 1950's and
1960's, Braine's formal education stopped in his middle teens.
The schooling which Braine received at St. Bede's, however, was
substantial; and, even though he took no certificate when he left
school in 1938, he graduated four years later after doing correspondence school work.

III *Librarian and Novelist*

After 1938, John Braine had jobs in a book shop, a furniture
store, a pharmaceutical laboratory, and a piston-ring factory.
After two years of such varied work, he became an assistant in
the Bingley, Yorkshire, Public Library. He remained a librarian,
with various interruptions, until 1957. One of the interruptions
was Braine's service as a telegrapher in the Royal Navy between
1940 and 1943, the year he was invalided out of the service because of tuberculosis. After he returned in 1943 to the Bingley
Public Library, he became chief assistant in 1949, a post which
he held for two years. In 1950, Braine moved to London and
worked as a free-lance writer until a serious bout with tuberculosis caused him to be hospitalized at Grassington between 1952
and 1954. Between 1950 and 1957 he published in *The New
Statesman* the six short sketches analyzed in Chapter 3.

After leaving the hospital in 1954, Braine took a position as
branch librarian in the Northumberland County Library—he had
become an associate of the Library Association in 1950. In 1956

Braine married Helen Patricia Wood, and the next year he returned to Yorkshire as branch librarian at the West Riding County Library, where he was employed when *Room at the Top* came out in 1957. With the publication and great success of his first novel, Braine again resigned from his position as librarian to devote himself to his writing of novels and of a few journalistic and autobiographical pieces. He mentions in the interview with Priestley that he gave five years of his life to a play that was never produced, and he says it "nearly lost me my life altogether." [8] I assume, therefore, that the work on the drama was done before 1952, when he had his last serious attack of tuberculosis.

Following the tremendous success of *Room at the Top*, Braine wrote *The Vodi* (1959), which was unsuccessful except among a few critics. In the first novel, Braine had concerned himself with the glossy success of a bright but poor young man. In the second book, he took a new tack and wrote about a young man who, like the author, had had a serious case of tuberculosis and had almost lost the will to live. The book, the most provincial of Braine's novels and the one most devoted to life in the lower classes, was marred by certain technical flaws and by a weakness of theme; but, as a picture of Yorkshire life before and after World War II, it is accurate and well done. Published in America under the title *From the Hand of the Hunter*, it achieved, as in England, little success. Between the two novels of the late 1950's, Braine for about four months wrote television reviews for *The Spectator;* but by then he was devoting most of his time to novels.

A third novel, *Life at the Top*, published in 1962, enjoyed a better sale than *The Vodi*. However, the critics were harsh and took the author to task for so obviously capitalizing in the sequel on the success of his first novel. The book had a much smaller sale than *Room at the Top*, and the American edition was remaindered in 1964 or 1965. But in 1965 a motion picture (again starring Laurence Harvey) was made of the novel. The reviews of the movie noted the falling-off from its predecessor, just as the novel itself had lost the immediacy of *Room at the Top*. Braine had been hailed as a promising young writer after the first two books, but *Life at the Top* caused several critics to feel that he had less talent than they had originally thought.

When *The Jealous God* was published in 1964, Braine's reputation recovered; his fourth novel was a critical success. An excellent novel, it proves the necessity of a novelist's serving an apprenticeship. Braine's first book was, in many ways, unfortunate in its success; it caused reviewers and critics to expect too much from him too soon. The other disappointing books offered him a chance to learn some things about structure and characterization, but the lessons were learned in the open, under the eyes of the reading world. The schooling was hard and the criticism severe. *The Jealous God* was evidence that Braine had come to maturity as a novelist, and it dispelled any fear that he was a one-novel writer.

Now a successful author, Braine lives in the community of Bingley, near Bradford but divorced from the most heavily in-dustrialized part of the area. He and his family live in a large Victorian house, but he maintains a flat in Bradford, where he goes daily to write. He works by a rigid schedule, writing from nine until twelve-thirty and from one-thirty until five. He makes up any lost time at night.[9]

He has avoided London since living there for a short time in 1950 and 1951. Braine prefers the North; in a radio talk pub-lished in *The Listener* he advanced his reasons. It is cheaper, for one thing: a house costing two thousand pounds in Bradford would cost twenty thousand in Mayfair. And, since he was born in the North, he feels that Bradford, where he is never "lionized," is the only place where he can carry on normal relationships with people who are not artists. And, while the landscape, he admits, is not beautiful, it is varied enough to satisfy him. The area suits Northerners so well, he says, that most wonder that Englishmen live elsewhere.[10]

IV   *John Braine and the "New Wave" of the English Novel*

Even though John Braine's first novel was published in 1957, it is necessary to go back at least to the beginning of that decade to understand something of the English literary climate that shaped his novels. The 1950's, called "the Angry Decade" [11] by Kenneth Allsop, ushered in a new generation of writers who altered—indeed, uprooted and overthrew—the traditions and practices of pre-war fiction. Most often the post-war writers are carelessly and inaccurately blanketed by the phrase "Angry Young Men," though most authors reject the term when it is ap-plied to them. And less popular are "the New Wave" and "the New Provincialism" that are used in describing some of the works of the 1950's.

Authors, for good reasons, always reject general terms that critics use to link them closely to other writers. For instance, no novelist wants to think of himself as belonging to "the Wain-Amis school"; certainly, no poet after World War I desired to think of himself, to use a popular term, as a "Wastelander." Therefore, any term which seems to limit a writer's uniqueness is rejected by him, and rightly so. No matter how appropriate an encompassing term is, it is almost certainly more convenient than accurate.

Some of the fictional movements in post-war English writing indicate the various ways in which John Braine's novels have been influenced by some of his contemporaries and related to others. As far as possible, the temptation to link Braine irrevocably and exclusively to a particular group of writers should be avoided; doing so would serve less purpose, I think, than a discussion of his individual qualities against a background of his times.

At the end of World War II there was no reigning English novelist in the sense that T. S. Eliot was an "agéd eagle," brooding over and dominating English poetry; but a good many novelists of the 1920's and 1930's were still alive. Aldous Huxley, Graham Greene, Evelyn Waugh, Henry Green, Joyce Cary, C. P. Snow, and Anthony Powell are perhaps the best-known names; and most of them are writing in the 1960's. Snow and Powell wrote their first novels in 1931 but established their reputations after the war. Huxley, of course, did his best work in the 1920's; and Greene did his in the following decade. Cary's best work was done in the 1940's—he died in 1957.

The majority of the writers on the pre-war literary scene constituted an Establishment—in the British sense of the word—in English letters. Most of them had been educated in public schools, then by Oxford or Cambridge, and were of upper- or upper-middle-class origins; Snow, a scholarship boy trained as a physicist, was an exception. (A writer with a background similar to D. H. Lawrence's had not made a name as a novelist in three decades.) The novels produced by the Establishment were, if set in England, likely to center around fashionable London or some country estate. Snow is again an exception, but not greatly so since some of his novels treat the lower middle classes in the provinces. Usually, though, his characters are dons or important figures in science and government.

For about five years after World War II, literature continued as it had before 1939; for the pre-war writers more or less took

up where they left off. There were, in any case, few novels published immediately following the war; the paper shortage often
caused a novel accepted for publication in 1945 to appear as
late as 1948.[12]

V *William Cooper*

Although the few first novels written before 1950 generally
tended to be in the pre-war tradition, William Cooper published
in 1950 a novel that had a far-reaching effect, despite its un-
obtrusive appearance on the scene. Called very simply *Scenes
From Provincial Life*, the novel centers around Joe Lunn and
his lower-middle-class friends who live in a small provincial
town far away from the great world of London. Most of the
characters are clerks or school teachers—Joe teaches half-heart-
edly in a dirty and poorly run state common school. There is no
glamor to life in the provinces; in fact, Joe and his friends plan
in 1939 to leave England for America, but war breaks out.
Cooper's book is realistic and deceptively commonplace. The
style is simple and underplayed, and the characters, while not
fully realized, are interesting because they reflect the quiet desperation of restless young men caught in the provinces on the
eve of the war.

Joe Lunn never became a celebrity character like Jim Dixon
in Kingsley Amis' *Lucky Jim* or Joe Lampton in *Room at the
Top*. In a great many ways, however, he is the forerunner of all
those anti-heroes with working-class first names who appear in
British fiction of the 1950's. The Jims, Joes, Jimmies, and Billies
who populate the new novels are a long way, in name as well as
in social status, from the Adams, Nicholases, and Sebastians of
pre-war fiction. Joe Lunn is merely the first of many dissatisfied,
frustrated young provincials seeking a way out of their situations.
The frustration of the characters in Waugh's novels, or Huxley's,
is personal; but that of the characters in the new novels is almost
always social. When Cooper's second Joe Lunn novel (set in
London ten years later) was published, Joe had become a successful civil servant and had lost by that time all his provincial
dissatisfaction. In that novel—titled *Scenes From Married Life*—
Joe is very much the man of the world who has achieved financial success and who no longer resembles the characters in the
other novels of "the angry decade," a decade which Cooper had
started in *Scenes From Provincial Life*. Between the two Joe
Lunn novels, Cooper wrote *The Young People*, which is also

concerned with the restlessness of working-class youth. The anti-hero is from a working-class background, but, until he is exposed, he passes himself off—even to his bride—as coming from a much higher class.

Cooper's importance lies not so much in any outstanding literary quality in his work as in the influence he had on a whole group of writers who wrote convincingly about life outside London—John Braine, Alan Sillitoe, Keith Waterhouse, David Storey, and others. Cooper showed that provincial life could be a fruitful, interesting source of novels, and that the London and manor-house novels were not the only ones that deserved a place in modern writing.

VI *Kingsley Amis*

In 1954 Kingsley Amis' first novel, *Lucky Jim*, revealed another facet of post-war literature that was to have a profound effect upon younger writers. Amis presents, with his character Jim Dixon, a distinctly new post-war type: a man educated in a Red Brick university who is irreverent toward all the traditions of the British Establishment. Dixon's irreverence takes the form of wildly humorous mockery of all that his elders and his betters hold sacred.

Jim Dixon, who has managed to become a tutor in history at a provincial university, finds during his first year that he hates the post, the university, and the whole academic profession. He sees everything connected with his university as hypocritical and disgusting; the head of his department, Professor Welch, is his particular symbol of all that is false. Welch is a clumsy, traditional old fool who goes in for madrigal singing, recorder playing, and the whole of what Jim regards as pseudo-intellectualism. Jim's war against the local Establishment is strictly a guerrilla campaign consisting of hilarious practical jokes and frustrated face-making when he is unobserved.

Jim's Chinese peasant's face, his Evelyn Waugh and Edith Sitwell faces, and his sex-life-in-Ancient-Rome face are all protests against the system and against his own cowardice for not getting out of the university: he works to gain tenure despite his detestation of everything academic. In fact, he chose history when he was a student because it was a notoriously easy course of study, rather than from any real interest in the subject. All occasions inform against him: his article—he must "publish or perish"—is stolen by an unscrupulous editor who publishes it later under his own name; he is chosen to give the year-end address to the university on the hilariously improbable subject, for a working-class youth, of Merrie England.

His academic career goes from bad to worse, until he is desperate, toward the end of the novel, for an escape from university life. His only hope lies in being selected as the private secretary to a man named Gore-Urquhart; and, when his prospective employer sees him making one of his absurd faces, Jim thinks all is lost. His Merrie England speech is his greatest disaster; for, having fortified himself with several drinks to calm himself, he is drunk when he gets up to speak. He hears his voice, as if from afar, imitating various local dignitaries as he begins to address the assembly; but he is powerless to stop himself until too much damage has been done. Of course, he is not able to continue in his post at the university; but Gore-Urquhart hires him. And he wins his girl—happily, he takes her away from Professor Welch's son.

Like John Braine's *Room at the Top*, *Lucky Jim* burst on the literary scene like a dropped bomb. The Establishment writers first praised the new turn that the novel was taking; but, upon greater reflection, they saw its mockery and the serious break with tradition that lay behind the uproariously funny doings of Amis' character. And there is no question that *Lucky Jim,* despite its apparently harmless humor, is a serious and bitter attack upon tradition.

Jim Dixon is the first of a long series of characters who are typically creatures of the post-war world. Though he and Braine's Joe Lampton are very different, both are products of the same disillusionment. In an earlier world—say in 1900—these nonheroes would have been excluded from university educations, and their activities would have been channeled into working-class occupations. If they had been particularly dissatisfied, they might have been followers of Keir Hardie in the Labour Movement. But the establishment of more universities and state scholarships allowed them to become educated. With an education, they were precluded from a working-class life but were still unacceptable, generally, to the Establishment.

The newer novelists of the 1950's saw the changing class structure from the viewpoint of the members of what someone has called the "new meritocracy." Anthony Powell's sequence of novels, *The Music of Time,* pictures this breakdown from the perspective of Nick Jenkins, an upper-class, Eton-Oxford, Establishment figure. Powell's version of Joe Lampton and Jim Dixon is the ludicrous Kenneth Widmerpool, who chooses assiduously (like Lampton) to climb upward in the Establishment. Widmerpool is a comic character whose comedy derives from his awkwardness in not being able to fit socially into a world of gentlemen. But Widmerpool, by sheer force of will, rises high in the business community, despite his cultural and social handicaps. The non-hero of the post-war novel has a decision to make because of his situation: he can, like Joe Lampton and Widmerpool, break into the world of "The Top"; he can react ironically and humorously as Jim Dixon does; or he can, like Jimmy Porter in Osborne's *Look Back in Anger*, resign from society and rail at it.

Amis' second novel, *That Uncertain Feeling*, treats a theme similar to that of *Lucky Jim* with a character not greatly different. The anti-hero of the second novel, John Lewis, is a disillusioned librarian in Wales who finally withdraws from the middle-class fray by returning to his native village, a coal-mining town, and by rejoining the working classes. Lewis finds the heartbreak of getting ahead and adjusting to a new culture too great a price to pay.

Only one other of Amis' novels—*Take a Girl Like You* (1960) —comes to grips with social problems. In that novel Jenny Bunn, a fresh-faced girl from the North, comes South to teach school and falls victim to an unscrupulous but not especially villainous seducer. When she loses her virtue while drunk, she is much less disturbed by the turn of events than she had thought she would be. Class, rural versus urban values, and mass culture come under scrutiny in this novel. The disillusionment is not so deep, it seems to me, as it is in *Lucky Jim* and in *That Uncertain Feeling*.

The whole concept of class is important in many ways to any consideration of the contemporary British novel. For the first time, a large number of authors are of working-class or lower-middle-class backgrounds; and much of their writing tends, naturally, to be about people like themselves or those whom they know well. And even the authors of the upper and upper middle classes frequently concern themselves with the changing class structure in post-war Britain. To understand the attitudes of the working classes in modern England is to understand, therefore, many of the bases of contemporary writing.

Richard Hoggart, a professor of English and a social critic, has written the best-known anatomy of the working-class mind and its problems in an age of mass culture. Titled *The Uses of*

Literacy,[13] Hoggart's book explores the whole problem faced by
the so-called lower orders. Hoggart, who comes from a working-
class background, knows acutely the problems of the Lucky
Jims and the Joe Lamptons who rise above their class and then
find that they are classless men in a structured society. Unacceptable to the university intellectuals and to the managerial
classes, they are also out of place, by virtue of their education,
among family and former friends. Hoggart does not discuss in
detail the social masks they wear, but the fiction writers do.
Amis has them rebel against society by mocking it; John Osborne has his anti-hero withdraw and scream insults at it;
Braine has Joe Lampton join it and out-do its members by becoming a thoroughgoing organization man.

The impact of Kingsley Amis' first novel is still being felt on
the English novel. *Lucky Jim* went through twenty impressions
in four years, was translated into nine languages, and has been
called one of the most "successful first novels in the English language." [14] His other novels have not enjoyed its success, but
several of the writers who were influenced by him have had
notable achievements. Some writers were influenced by his humor
and others by his delineation of social problems in welfare-state
England. Braine, for instance, was much less affected by Amis'
humor than was Keith Waterhouse, a Yorkshireman, whose *Billy
Liar* is a novel about an adolescent Lucky Jim. Amis' importance,
insofar as it is confined to influence upon other writers, lies in
his showing the way for the novel of revolt and protest and in
his recognizing a social fact that confronts post-war England.
Most important, though, he is a writer of merit and of im-
mense comic talent, whose novels need no apology.

VII   *John Osborne*

John Osborne, not a novelist but a playwright, has had such
a far-reaching influence on post-war literature that a discussion of his works is necessary to an understanding of the decade
that produced Joe Lampton. His play *Look Back in Anger* was
produced in London in 1956, and the opening night was one of
the most shocking in London stage history. After being fed a
diet of imitation Noel Coward for a good many years, the audience found from *Look Back in Anger* that life still existed in
the drama in England. But more important, at least in considering its effect on literature, the play introduced Jimmy Porter,
who is truly an "Angry Young Man." In fact, many people

credit Osborne with inventing the phrase, though it was first used in 1951 as the title of an autobiography by Leslie Paul.[15]

Jimmy Porter and his creator became symbols for the entire revolutionary spirit of the mid-1950's. Porter lives in a small flat with his wife, Alison, and his friend Cliff Lewis. The first act opens on Sunday, a day devoted by Jimmy to reading the papers and to railing at society. He and Cliff run a small candy store in a working-class district; and Alison, the daughter of a former army colonel, stagnates in unfamiliar surroundings. Porter constantly reviles Alison for her high-caste background, for to him she carries on her head all the evils of the Establishment. But to describe Jimmy Porter merely as an anti-Establishment "Angry Young Man" is only to tell part of the story. He is angry at the world, which he feels is dead. He complains that there are no causes any more and that the world is much more likely to end with a whimper than a bang.

Jimmy Porter is not a typical product of the Welfare State, but he has much in common with the scholarship boys of Amis. He attended a university (not even, in his case, red brick, but white tile, the lowest kind). He was unable to adjust to the scholarship boys' world or even to carry on a mocking attack like Jim Dixon. Instead, he has rejoined the working class by running his shop in a run-down part of a Midlands town. His anger at the state of British society is no greater than his anger at the whole "dead" world. His hate takes the form of breath-taking tirades against Alison, her family, the press, the American way, and his own impoverished childhood. The play is less a drama than a sustained frenzy by Jimmy. He builds himself up to one assault after another until the audience is utterly exhausted by the fury of his attacks.

The author, who also wrote *The Entertainer*, a play concerned with the spiritually dead man in the modern world, was, at the time, at least as angry as his characters. This anger is evident in the essay that Osborne contributed to *Declaration*,[16] a collection of essays by post-war writers of the Colin Wilson-John Wain stamp. The purpose of *Declaration* was to provide a forum so that some of the young writers could express "themselves in their own particular fields ... and define their positions in relation to society today."[17] Osborne's essay amounted to an attack upon royalty—"the gold filling in a mouthful of decay";[18] upon the political Establishment; and upon the Church—"It has lived in an atmosphere of calm, casual funk. .... It has even managed to spread the gospel of funk."[19] There is very little in modern

Britain that Osborne does not find corrupt, but he considered
the application of the phrase "Angry Young Man" to be a journalistic trick.

There is no arguing that Osborne had a tremendous influence
on the climate of literary opinion in the 1950's. His play *Look
Back in Anger*—his other plays have not been so impressive—
and his journalistic endeavors helped to shape the thought of
the period. The man who, like Jimmy Porter, has been killed by
society is a central theme of the writing of the decade. This
theme is also dealt with by John Braine in *Room at the Top*
and in *Life at the Top*, and Braine uses the term "Zombie" (the
walking dead) to characterize the deadened man. However,
Braine does not altogether follow the Osborne line; he makes
Joe as responsible for his own spiritual death as society is, while
Jimmy's own contribution to his hollowness is not revealed fully.

Osborne's life, unlike Amis' or Wain's, is almost a paradigm
of the life of an "Angry Young Man." Born into a working-class
family—his grandmother was retired on a pension from Wool-
worth's and his mother worked behind the bar in a pub[20]—Osborne attended school until he was sixteen, took a short turn as
a journalist on *The Gas World*, and then spent ten years as an
actor in a repertory company. He was either acting two plays
a night for two pounds a week or subsisting on the welfare dole.[21]
His brilliant play, *Look Back in Anger*, is probably founded on
the financial and social frustration that he had known until he
reportedly earned twenty thousand pounds from his first play.[22]
I mention the facts of his life only because he is very explicit
about them in his journalistic writings and uses them to show
how he has been formed as a human being and a writer. His
life became as important as his plays to many commentators,
and the biographical details that he discusses so interestingly in
his essay in *Declaration* helped shape the literary model of the
"Angry Young Man."

VIII   *John Wain*

Mistaking John Wain and John Braine is quite frequent among
casual readers, more, I am sure, because their names sound alike
than because their writings are similar. Yet the influence of Wain
upon Braine is considerable; in fact, Wain's influence on the
fiction of the 1950's and 1960's is very great, though it is difficult
to estimate the role that he has played solely as a novelist; for
he has also functioned significantly as a poet, a journalist, and a

literary critic. It is, perhaps, in the last two pursuits that he has been most influential; yet his first novel, *Hurry on Down,* published in 1953, is almost prehistorical in the history of the "Angry Decade." Although *Hurry on Down* was published before *Lucky Jim* (1954), it did not have the influence of *Lucky Jim* and *Look Back in Anger,* probably the two most important works of the decade.

When *Hurry on Down* was published by Secker and Warburg in 1953 (it was issued in America in 1954 under the title *Born in Captivity*), the English reviews were mixed, a few hostile; and it took several years for it to sell ten thousand copies. Wain disagrees with Colin Wilson's *Encounter* article which said that the book sold very well and received rave reviews.[23] A good many American critics, apparently following Wilson's lead, spoke of the rave reviews of *Hurry on Down;* but, as Wain has pointed out, they did not exist. The book did not have anything like the impact of *Lucky Jim,* published a few months later. Over the years, Wain has become in the eyes of journalists a sort of archetypal "Angry Young Man"; writers surveying the literary history of the 1950's have credited Wain with a great deal of early influence. And doubtless he had some, but only in a quiet way during the first three or four years of his career.

Hurry on Down is not an even novel, but it has many interesting features, one of which is its treatment of the class structure. The main character, Charles Lumley, abandons his own class after he leaves the university to become, in rapid succession, a window washer, a professional driver, a smuggler, a hospital orderly, a chauffeur, and a radio-gag writer. Seeking a life based on something more worth while than the artificial values of the commercial classes, he joins the working classes; however, he never is able to become a member except superficially—he can never do more than earn his living in the same way that they do. Never able to join himself to any class, he early realizes—and this is the theme of the book—that the individual and his own values are more important than any badges of class. The university has prepared him to be a snob like his classmate Hutchins; it has fitted him only for the life of a pedant; therefore, he abandons all for which education has prepared him.

Lumley really tries several times to become a member of the mindless working classes: he is once on the point of marrying Rose, who has a menial job in a hospital and whose father reads *News of the World* on Sunday and dozes by the fire. But it is just as impossible for Lumley to be like Rose's father as it is

for him to imitate the stolid Hutchins. He finally finds that only
by becoming a member of a comic's stable of writers can he
seek individual values and still submerge himself in a thoroughly
mindless occupation, the absurdity of which helps give him individual perspective. The American title *Born in Captivity* is
more revealing of Charles Lumley's plight; near the end of the
book, it is observed that a bird born in captivity will die or be
killed if he is released among wild birds. Charles is almost killed
by the world; he barely is able to avoid death (physical and
moral) several times. The captivity of his birth was social and
class dictated.

Wain's second novel, *Living in the Present* (1955), differs from
his other novels in some ways; but its theme—that one must
find his own meanings—runs throughout Wain's novels and
short stories. Edgar Banks, the hero, decides at the beginning
to kill himself; but first he decides to rid the world of the
worst person whom he can think of. He selects an Anglo-Catholic
rightist as his victim and follows him all over Europe before he
finds that he is unable to kill either Philipson-Smith or himself.
Edgar, while planning to kill himself, is living wholly in the
present; but, when he finds that he does not have to expect the
impossible from life to be happy with what it offers, he begins
to live in the future. On the last page of the novel, he realizes
that happiness is within his reach if he will relax and quit prov-
ing himself. Happiness will come, Banks thinks, a little at a
time; he is amazed that he ever planned suicide as "he thought
of the bad yesterdays and the wonderful to-morrows. . . . He was
tired of living in the present." [24]

This novel was unsuccessful for several reasons. Wain said, in
the 1960 preface to the American edition, that his plot was too
mechanical and that he followed it too slavishly. The book, he
says, ran into a marsh half-way through and did not regain pace
until the end.[25] The reviewers treated the book badly, and its
sales were poor. It, again, had little impact on the times. But
the third novel, *The Contenders* (1958), is much better than the
first two and added to Wain's reputation as a novelist. By the
time of its publication, however, he was already a well-known
journalist and literary critic. For his essays on literature—published as *Preliminary Essays* and as *Essays on Literature and
Ideas*—established him as a most promising new practical critic.

Wain's *The Contenders* is the story of a trio of provincial
youths who go separate ways in the world in their attempt to
find what they value in life. Narrator Joe Shaw finds his happi-

ness by remaining in the provincial town that bred him and by being a newspaper man. Joe witnesses and reports the lives of Ned Roper and Robert Lamb, both of whom are "contenders." Lamb, an artist, leaves his home to go to London, where he loses creativity. Ned becomes an industrialist and a success in life; but Joe, like Edgar Banks, learns to live a day at a time without constantly contending and is the only real success.

Wain's purpose in the novel is to "tackle the problem," he says, of the corrupting nature of material ambition and rivalry, to discuss the value of work, and to explore metropolitan versus provincial virtues: "being in touch versus sturdy independence." [26] He chooses the provinces against the brilliant vacuity of the city. In many ways, Wain is as provincial a writer as Cooper or Braine. In fact, Robert Weaver—who divides some of the writers of the 1950's into mystics, provincials, and radicals—considers as provincials Wain, Braine, and Amis (Osborne is a radical; Colin Wilson, a mystic).[27]

The Contenders is a better novel than the first two by Wain because it allows the theme to grow naturally from the characters, while both the early books attempted to illustrate a thesis. Wain's fourth novel, *A Travelling Woman* (1959), is mainly concerned with happiness as it is found in sexual relationships. Every character in the novel is seeking some sort of fulfillment, and most are entangled in illicit sexual alliances. George Links, the main character, realizes too late that, to find contentment, he should have been true to his wife. The theme is the same in the other novels—one needs to reassess his own moral values and find a code to live by. James Gindin says that *The Contenders* and *A Travelling Woman* are both socially oriented to an extent that Wain's other novels are not, and that in them "contemporary society is rejected in favor of the value of an older, more local, tradition." [28]

One characteristic of Wain that I have omitted in my discussion is his humor. All the novels are funny, and a number of patterns of humor are explored. Wain has a gift for parody and farce, but in the early novels, the farce often obtrudes upon the seriousness of the themes.

Wain is an all-purpose man of letters[29] in a way that no one else writing today in England is. He has two volumes of poetry, two of criticism, five novels, an autobiography, and numerous uncollected essays. In *Declaration*, he states his general intellectual position, which seems borne out in the substance of his novels. His view of man's plight in this century is different from many of his contemporaries. He says that there are few intellectual changes that do not go back at least to the turn of the century; but, until the 1950's, man could be modern merely by vaguely accepting progress and new ideas. The present generation (those who came to maturity in the 1950's) has to confront the key ideas of modern life and is unable to get by "on mere enthusiastic acceptance."[30] Modern man is on a tightrope— Wain's essay is called "Along the Tightrope"—and must keep his head by rejecting "wholesale thinking."[31] He cannot afford charlatanism; therefore, he must reject the elders who jeer at his lack of commitment and go step by step along the tightrope.[32]

Although devoting so much space to a discussion of Wain may seem inappropriate, his impact on the decade, when we consider his various kinds of writing, has been tremendous. And there is also much in John Braine that seems to come directly from Wain; in fact, few of his contemporaries are untouched by his ideas and practices; they are either in agreement with or in reaction against them. Kenneth Allsop considers Wain's reputation as much more inflated than even Colin Wilson's but as much less vulnerable to criticism because it was established in highbrow circles: "Wain is undoubtedly the most over-rated writer of the Fifties, and stands as a lesson in present-day careerism— how, if he is aggressive enough about it, a writer can get himself accepted at his own evaluation, irrespective of talent."[33] Needless to say, I disagree.

IX Colin Wilson

One of the new wave of writers Braine discussed in his American lectures was Colin Wilson, who, for a time, was one of the intellectual leaders of the new fiction in England. Like Braine, he reacted against the in-bred nature of English writing and culture, though in a far different way.

Wilson's reputation was inflated in the first decade of his work, but with the coming of the 1960's, his writings have been more accurately valued. In 1956, he published *The Outsider* (written by day in the British Museum while the author slept on Hampstead Heath at night) in which he attacks the decline of Western civilization. Certain outsiders, among whom are Friedrich Nietzsche, T. E. Lawrence, Waslaw Nijinski, Jean-Paul Sartre, Albert Camus, Sören Kierkegaard, Fyodor Dostoyevsky, and Vincent Van Gogh, are pointed to as examples of men who have resisted the ravages of civilization. The "outsider" stands for

truth and individuality against the pressures of a society that
seeks to integrate all men into its mediocrity. But the "outsider"
cannot live in the world of the middle classes; for, while he sees
the world as chaos, they see it as order. For him, the world is
neither rational nor orderly; and *"truth must be told at all costs,*
otherwise there can be no hope for an ultimate restoration of
order." [34]

This attack upon convention stirred many of the world's young
intellectuals, who agreed that the great evil was conformity. For
one year, Wilson was flattered and hailed as a genius by what
seemed to be the whole world. But, when *Religion and the Rebel,*
the second half of *The Outsider,* appeared in 1957, the second
look that everyone took caused his reputation as a sage to plum-
met. In 1955 Kenneth Allsop devoted several pages[35] to tracing
the interesting rise and fall of Colin Wilson; however, Wilson
had published only two books then. He has since published
about a dozen others—five novels, a book of music criticism, a
volume of autobiography, and four volumes of what his agent's
blurb calls "The Outsider Cycle." All these books met with
either cool or hostile receptions, and Wilson today is the nine-
day wonder whose impact upon the times was intense but brief.

His importance, nevertheless, was as a "philosopher" for the
new wave of the English novel; and he said in his own original,
if haphazard, way much that needed saying about the burden-
some conformity of post-war society. He put into angry words
what many of the young writers vaguely felt and had dramatized,
or were to dramatize, in fiction and plays. He cried out for a
return to a religion of sorts, for he feels that man needs a saviour
(perhaps a Nietzschean or Shavian superman) to lead him out
of the wilderness of chaos. Wilson's statement of the twentieth-
century problem is interesting and valuable; his remedy is, however, unacceptable.

But Wilson was right in seeing man as trapped in a rational-
appearing state of chaos. He saw that he could retreat into conformity (as Joe Lampton does) or become an "outsider" and
make his own rules. In other words, as Arthur Schlesinger, Jr.
puts it in discussing youth's choices, some "sought security at the
expense of identity and became organization men. Others sought
identity at the expense of security and became beatniks." [36] Joe
Lampton is a case of a man taking the first course; Jim Dixon,
the second. Either course results in the creation of a partial
man.[37]

32   JOHN BRAINE

X *Stuart Holroyd and Bill Hopkins*

Two other writers often linked to Wilson are Stuart Holroyd and Bill Hopkins. Hopkins wrote a much-beleaguered novel—*The Divine and the Decay* (1957)—that recounted the rise of a Nietzschean superman who is a latter-day Fascist. Since Wilson and Hopkins were friends, Wilson praised *The Divine and the Decay* extravagantly. Other critics, however, thought the book a boring story of a tin-horn tyrant; and Hopkins has no reputation today.

Holroyd's *Emergence From Chaos* (1957) calls for a return to religion to help lead man out of chaos. The book is not influenced by Wilson; in fact, Wilson read Holroyd's manuscript before writing *The Outsider*. *Emergence From Chaos* studies six poets—T. S. Eliot, W. B. Yeats, Arthur Rimbaud, Rainer Maria Rilke, Walt Whitman, and Dylan Thomas—who used religion as a way out of chaos. These poets exemplify Holroyd's own thesis that religion alone—any kind of religion, as I understand it—will help to unify man's life. He shows, he says, how the modern poets "have succeeded in emerging from the chaos into which they were plunged by the accident of their birth." [38]

Holroyd's book seems to me a more reasoned and unified study than Wilson's *The Outsider,* and it has stood the test of a decade much better. Since it studies the works of the writers in some detail, it is valid as a document of literary criticism in a way that Wilson's is not; yet its influence on the writers of the 1950's and 1960's is considerably less.

XI *Thomas Hinde*

Only one other writer of the 1950's who antedates Braine is important in showing the drift of the British novel: Thomas Hinde, whose novel *Happy as Larry* (1957) is one of the best books of the decade. In 1953 he had published *Mr. Nicholas,* a book which achieved a great but limited critical success. *Mr. Nicholas* is a first-rate novel about a middle-class, retired Tory who lives in a suburb of London and tries to uphold all the values of Imperial England. But he is as unable to hold his family—a wife and three sons—together as Britain was to keep her Empire. There is a sense of defeat and decay about the whole novel: Mr. Nicholas is having an affair with a horrid woman, one son runs off with a homosexual, and one is verging on rebellion. The old England is over; the tennis, the cricket club, and the

Defend Britain Club that Mr. Nicholas starts—all are futile attempts to resurrect a world that had passed away long ago. The novel is devastating in an understated way; not a word is out of place and not once does the author allow himself to rant, moan, or deplore the awful unreality of the Nicholas family and its way of life.

Hinde—the author's real name is Sir Thomas Chitty—brought out his second novel, *Happy as Larry*, the same year that Braine published *Room at the Top*. The two novels show opposite sides of Schlesinger's coin—Joe trades identity for security; Larry Vincent forfeits security to become a beatnik. And then, with security gone, he loses his identity. He is one of the closest parallels in the decade to Samuel Beckett's doomed men.[39]

When Larry Vincent watches his wife run down by a truck, he doesn't try to help; for some reason, he is unable to do anything but keep an appointment with a seedy pervert. Larry assumes that his wife is dead, but twenty-four hours or so later he learns that she is alive and is going to be taken back by parents who have decided that she cannot be entrusted any longer to Larry. As Larry mentally disintegrates, he begins a strange, futile, and sometimes hilarious search for a compromising photograph of one of his friends. His rounds lead him back to his wife's family, who throw him out, to a bizarre relationship with a girl as sick as he is, to meetings with all kinds of fellow sufferers from the disease of modernism. Larry Vincent moves from horror to hell and, finally, back merely to horror. There is some slight note of hope at the end; but, as Allsop points out, comparatively, Wain's and Amis' heroes "are living on the sunny side of the street." [40] Hinde's first two novels, though almost unknown in America, rank with *Lucky Jim, Room at the Top*, and *Billy Liar* as the most impressive writing of the 1950's.

So far, we have discussed writers of the 1950's who predated Braine and who either influenced him or wrote out of similar convictions about the spirit of the times. My general plan has been to show a series of developments in post-war fiction up to the publication of *Room at the Top* in 1957. I have, doubtless, overlooked writers of merit, some on purpose and some accidentally. Many writers who wrote in the period were either holdovers from an earlier time or writers whose development seems to me to be in a direction different from the authors I have concentrated on. For instance, Iris Murdoch used to be discussed as a member of the Amis-Wain axis; but I have never felt her to be very much like the writers I have been discussing.

Her first novel, *Under the Net* (1954), has a central figure who
superficially resembles the lost figures of the 1950's. But her development has been uniquely oriented toward personal traits of
characters, and a discussion of her is irrelevant to the more social
orientation of Amis, Wain, Braine, and the others.

The writers who came after Braine but who wrote (and write)
in the same vein, need to be considered briefly if anything like
a total picture of the English social and provincial novel in
Braine's era is to be presented. Three other novelists, who published first novels about the time Braine did or later, serve to
complete the picture: Keith Waterhouse, Alan Sillitoe, and David
Storey. Sillitoe and Waterhouse are better known, but all three
are most talented.

XII   *Keith Waterhouse*

Waterhouse's first novel, almost forgotten today, is good
enough to merit some consideration. Titled *There Is a Happy
Land* (1957), the novel traces a few months in the life of an
orphaned pre-teen boy who lives with his aunt in a state-run,
low-rent housing district. Told entirely from the third-grader's
point of view, the novel gives a valid picture of North Country
life before World War II as it was seen by a small, unloved
boy. The best part of the novel, as a matter of fact, is the regional picture: the games children play; the retorts they make;
the language they speak; and the descriptions of the fields
around the factories, the government housing, the national school,
and the streets where children play—all are well done and
show Waterhouse's promise as a novelist. The children skulk
about the warehouse of the Clerk of the Works; they hide in
dugouts in the fields; they explore quarries and culverts. The
church fairs, the home-made amusements, the nicknames, and
the importance of movies and comics are all acutely felt by the
narrator and by the reader. The influence of the post-war provincial writers is clearly in evidence in *There Is a Happy Land;*
and, while the book is not excellent, it is adequate and indicates
a more than sufficient talent.

The little boy—his name is never told—is a witness to, and
participant in, many events which he does not understand but
which the reader does. Uncle Mad, an apparent homosexual, is
a constant menace to the children, and the narrator is almost
caught by him. Finally, his little playmate is murdered in a
sex crime and everyone assumes that Uncle Mad killed her, but

it turns out that Big Rayner, a boy a year or two older than the narrator, was the killer. The little boy who sees and relates the action of the novel is beset by psychological problems resulting from his being an orphan ridiculed by the other children. His daydreaming, his tendency to lie and to rationalize his lies, and his futile search for acceptance are all well rendered. Waterhouse's novels are by no means, therefore, mere regional color stories. His second and third novels are interesting both as psychological studies and as reflections of provincial life; but *Billy Liar* is one of the outstanding provincial studies of the post-war period.

Billy Liar, published in 1959, is an end-of-decade *Lucky Jim.* The novel relates one day in the life of Billy Fisher—the liar of the title and the narrator. Billy, an adolescent who lives and works in the West Riding of Yorkshire, is thoroughly disillusioned about the life there. There are two sides to life that he cannot abide: one is the Americanized milk-bar existence; the other, the phoney provincial, represented by Man o' the Dales, a local newspaper columnist who writes about the quaintness of Old Yorkshire. The milk-bar group consists of Billy's friends, frustrated young men like himself. Billy, who is engaged to a waitress in the milk-bar, is also engaged to a tweedy, healthy girl of Old Yorkshire. His real interest, though, is a third girl, Liz, who is just herself. The phoney Yorkshire appears not only in Man o' the Dales but in all the people who affect the broad dialect and who are interested in arts, crafts, and folklore of the shire. The two girls engaged to Billy represent the two sides of Yorkshire that he finds most repugnant.

Billy Fisher normally finds his escape from the awfulness of life by inventing a land called "Ambrosia," where he is the national hero. In place of his drab working-class parents, he invents a noble couple called "mater" and "pater." He also finds escape by lying to people who do not know him (and to people who do) about a sister he does not have and about numerous other facts of his life. His ambition is to become a television performer and writer; he plans, just before the end of the book, to run away to London to work for an entertainment personality who has vaguely promised to give him an audition; to Billy, the promise is a guarantee of a job. Toward the end of the book, all his deceptions are revealed—his two fiancées; his failure to mail a number of calendars that the funeral parlor where he works had earlier entrusted to him; and, indeed, his whole tendency to deceive people.

The book is two things: a devastatingly satiric picture of life
in a drab, phoney, Americanized provincial town; an interesting
and, I think, accurate exploration of the mind of a disturbed
adolescent. The satire is directed at the whole provincial pattern
of dullness, pretention, and imitation. Billy dislikes all the things
one has to do to get ahead in Stradhoughton; he also dislikes the
made-up traditions and the copying of American customs, dress,
and slang. He is no reformer; he just wants to escape the vicious
pattern of life by running away to London or to Ambrosia.

As a psychological study, the book is concerned with all the
things an adolescent has to endure. His parents are hopelessly
ignorant and uninterested in him. From time to time, when his
father screams out that he is not having Billy stay out all night,
Billy wants to reply by asking who he *is* having stay out. The
grandmother, whose death prevents Billy's escape at the end of
the novel, is a hapless old woman whose senility is a burden to
all. Billy's employers, like his girl friends, represent the two sides
of provincial life that he hates. The younger employer, thoroughly Americanized, keeps a copy of Evelyn Waugh's *The
Loved One* in his desk, not for amusement, but as a source of
good ideas about the undertaking business. The older employer,
Councilor Duxbury, is a bluff, hearty Old Yorkshire type, who
speaks in the broad dialect. Billy mocks both of them to their
faces, but he is startled when old Duxbury finally points out to
him that he has recognized the mocking all along. Duxbury is
the more humane and sensible, for, when Billy's deception about
the calendars is discovered, he is not unreasonable.

For a devastatingly accurate picture of the worst aspects of
provincial life, there is no better post-war novel than Waterhouse's *Billy Liar*. His third novel, *Jubb* (1963), also a success,
is narrated by the most disturbed of Waterhouse's three nar-
rators. C. L. Jubb—a *voyeur*, a fetishist, and an arsonist—lives
in a state-developed suburb about halfway between London and
Cambridge. During the two weeks or so of the novel's action,
Jubb completely degenerates; when he leaves Chapel Lantry
(his town), he has burned down the neighborhood center at
which he had recently been deposed as a counselor.

The novel's main interest is in the abnormal psychology of
its central character. The reader, who sees that Jubb's perver-
sions completely control him, is allowed to hear Jubb rationalize
them. Jubb sees nothing very strange in what he does; in those
instances where he knows his behavior to be asocial, he rea-
sonably defends his actions. By the end of the book, Jubb has

become completely psychotic, and the reader has been acutely and believingly in attendance. What the child narrator of *There Is a Happy Land* and Billy Fisher are capable of becoming, Jubb has become. In fact, his early life is much like that of the child in Waterhouse's first novel—both parents are dead, and he and his brother (who may have caused the fire in which the parents died) live with an aunt in a run-down neighborhood.

The setting of *Jubb*, as of all of Waterhouse's books, is an integral part. The whole weakness of welfare-state subdivision is brought under scrutiny. The row houses on streets like Apple Croft, Peach Croft, and Cherry Croft are deadly in their sameness. The Neighborhood Committees and their parliamentary pedantry are sharply drawn. The petty bickering of lower-class and lower-middle-class neighbors is excoriated. While *Jubb* is not exactly provincial in the way that *Billy Liar* is, it does present a satiric view of suburbanism in the new bureaucracy.

Waterhouse has also written a series of plays in collaboration with Willis Hall, but they were all roundly denounced in the British weeklies. Apparently Waterhouse's forte is the novel, for his three novels have so far been critically successful; and the last two drew considerable attention. Waterhouse is still a very young writer—he was born in 1933 in Yorkshire—and is talented enough to become a first-rate figure in English letters.

XIII   Alan Sillitoe

Far more class oriented than Braine or Waterhouse is Alan Sillitoe, whose *Saturday Night and Sunday Morning* (1958), *The Loneliness of the Long Distance Runner* (1960), and *Key to the Door* (1962) treat proletarian life in the industrial midlands. A fourth novel, *The General* (1960), is a political allegory set in an unnamed country at a time when the "cold war" has become a hot one.

Saturday Night and Sunday Morning (1958) was one of those first novels, like *Lucky Jim* and *Room at the Top*, which captured the essence of the times and became a literary sensation. Thoroughly proletarian, the novel is a chronicle of a short period in the life of Arthur Seaton, a man of twenty-two who works as a lathe operator in a bicycle factory. His whole life is a series of Saturday nights and Sunday mornings—drunks and hangovers. His work is so dulling that he lives only for the pleasures, often illicit, of the weekend. The novel is, in short, a depressing study of the modern technological world and what it

does to the workers in it. But it is more: it is also a penetrating
study of proletarian morals and values, as revealed in Arthur.
Moreover, it is a very accurate picture of the provincial Notting-
ham equivalent of Braine's Dead Dufton and Warley.

Arthur Seaton is an "angry young man," but not in the same
way that Amis' characters or Wain's are; he is angry in the
older tradition of the early Lawrence and George Orwell.
Arthur—an anarchist who hates Tories, Liberals, and Labourites
—says he would like to see the Houses of Parliament auctioned
off for sixpence a chance. His whole world is seen in terms of
"them" and "us," but his dissatisfaction is less with abstract
politics than with things that touch his own narrow, hedonistic
existence. He sees nothing in his past but the dole of the 1930's
that made his parents miserable—Sillitoe returns to that world
for about two hundred pages of Key to the Door—and there is
nothing in the future but death. Arthur says: "Factories sweat
you to death, labour exchanges talk you to death; insurance and
income-tax offices milk money from your wage packets and rob
you to death. . . . the army calls you up and you get shot to
death" (220). As a result of his view, Arthur lives for the
present; he buys fancy clothes and carries on affairs with two
sisters (both of whom are married) until he is caught. He makes
no plans beyond Saturday night until almost the end of the
novel; then he finally decides to take a chance and marry.

Two things are interesting about the novel: the angry, proletarian world and the brilliantly drawn sketch of Nottinghamshire
working life. The whole novel is colored by the hazy, murky
atmosphere of the drab Midlands. The scenes in the factory in
which Arthur "works his guts out" and in the various working-
class pubs are marvelously realistic. The Christmas scene at his
Aunt Ada's is brilliantly done, for it dramatizes the sort of great
family party that John Osborne talks about in the essay in
Declaration. Sillitoe's whole picture of working-class life seems
almost a fictionalization of Richard Hoggart's book about the
working classes—The Uses of Literacy.

Not only are the descriptions of Midland life accurate and
real, but Sillitoe has, along with Waterhouse, a great ear for dialogue. We never feel that Sillitoe's characters, unlike those of
Braine, are overdoing the dialect. The masterful grasp of spoken
language that Sillitoe displays is nowhere better seen than in the
title story from his book of short stories, The Loneliness of the
Long Distance Runner. The story is a first-person narrative by
a reformatory boy named Smith, who is being trained by the

institution to be a long distance runner and to win a cup by racing against boys from other reformatories. He trains assiduously, but he is determined to lose the race in order to embarrass the governor and the "pig faced" ladies and gentlemen on the reviewing stand. He loses very obviously by slowing down to a walk right at the finish line. His failure causes his last six months in jail to be miserable, for the governor assigns every dirty job that he can think of to Smith.

Smith sees the whole struggle between himself and society as a "we-them" engagement. When the governor of the prison entreats him to become honest, he sees his own fidelity to class and his own hatred of those above him as a much higher honesty. There is no reforming of Smith, who plans to go out into society and continue his life of crime. At the end of the story he reports that he has just stolen six hundred and twenty-eight pounds. He is not especially bitter about prison; for, as he says, "I lost the governor's race all right, and won my own twice over . . ." (53). Moreover, his stay in the reformatory steeled him for his trade and gave him the pleurisy that keeps him out of the army.

Sillitoe's third novel, *Key to the Door,* is partly set in Nottinghamshire and partly in Malaya where Brian Seaton is in the army helping to put down the Communist guerrillas. Brian, Arthur's brother, refuses to shoot a Chinese Communist, who is a man and therefore more akin to Brian than the British officers and government are. This kinship that he feels—Arthur almost feels it once or twice—is apparently his key to the door of life.

The first half of the novel is interesting in showing the rigors of life on the dole during the 1930's. Arthur, in *Saturday Night and Sunday Morning,* is almost too young to remember the Seatons' poverty; but he is firmly convinced that the mindless drinking, smoking, and "telly" watching of the 1950's is preferable. After reading about the Seatons of the 1930's, the reader is convinced that, despite the degradations of post-war life, the working classes of the 1950's are better off.

Alan Sillitoe is a powerful novelist, and the anger that bursts from *The Loneliness of the Long Distance Runner, Saturday Night and Sunday Morning* and *Key to the Door* is in no way a sham; it is deeply felt. His power, the quality that is most impressive about his novels, reminds me of D. H. Lawrence, who was also from Nottinghamshire. There is something, perhaps, in Midlands life that causes writers to feel and write powerfully. Both *Sons and Lovers* and *Saturday Night and Sunday Morning*

give an indication of the harshness of working-class life that
molds forceful writers.

XIV   David Storey

A younger Yorkshire contemporary of Braine's is David Storey
(born 1933), whose three novels have provincial settings. The
first of his novels, *This Sporting Life* (1960), has a history similar to that of the first novels of Braine, Sillitoe, and Amis—large
sales, good reviews, and successful movies made from them.
This Sporting Life is about Arthur Machin, a professional rugby
player in an industrial town in Yorkshire. The best part of the
novel is the squalid picture presented of the rough world of
rugby football. All this—the value struggle, the squalor, the
crassness—is set against a well-drawn provincial environment
that gives the novel a clear sense of setting. Storey's use of setting in his first novel is almost as impressive as Braine's.

Machin comes from the poorer, lower middle class; but his
football playing puts him, for the first time, into the income
bracket where he can drive a Jaguar and have plenty of money
to spend. His parents, who represent the values of an older
generation, are disturbed both by what Arthur has to do to make
money and by how he spends it. His mistress, Valerie Hammond,
is from a working-class background; and her distaste at Arthur's
flashiness stems from her own mistrust of the values of "them"
as distinct from the "us" of the stricter and, in some ways, more
reserved lower orders. Class differences are at the center of the
novel; in fact, they are central in all of Storey's fiction. He uses
the clash between the segments of society as the catalytic principle in each of his three novels. That class differences are frequently responsible for the struggles between people and genera-
tions is made clear in Storey's second novel—*Flight into Camden*
(1961).

Told from the point of view of Margaret Thorpe, the novel
relates the conflict among her, her brother, and their father over
what matters in life; and a similar struggle occurs between Margaret and a married man with whom she runs away. The father,
a coal miner, had educated his two children much above his
own station: one becomes a lecturer in a university; the other,
a secretary with a middle-class outlook. When Margaret brings
a man to spend the weekend in the family home, located in a
mining development, while the rest of the family is away, the
parents react violently and predictably. They cannot stand the

censure of their working-class neighbors, nor can they bear to think that their own daughter is involved with a married man. Margaret and Howarth, her lover, flee to Camden Town, a suburb of London, where they try to lose themselves among the faceless masses of that city. Howarth, a weak and uncertain man, perhaps because of his classlessness, is an artist turned teacher. He attempts to win Margaret over to his own muddy, uncertain view of life, greatly to her detriment. The father and mother, who become physically ill at her defection, try to force Margaret to return. The brother, whose working-class orientation is stronger than his father had thought, becomes as outraged as the parents and actually tries to drag her back. When Howarth finally leaves her because he knows that she can never be as he is, she returns home; and he, a little later, returns to his wife.

The point of the novel, I think, is that the marks of class which one acquires early are harder to lose than they seem, and that a person can only be happy in conforming to the background that formed his character. Howarth can never be a complete man because he has no root beliefs and no class orientation to sustain him. Arthur Machin's problem is that, when he sells himself for money, he destroys any genuine connections in his life. He is not at home with his parents, with Valerie, or with the owners of the team who lead him on socially and then drop him.

Radcliff (1963), Storey's third novel, while it uses class distinctions and a provincial setting, is quite far from the novels I have been discussing in this chapter. The novel's main character is Leonard Radcliff, whose father is caretaker of an estate that was once the seat of the Radcliff family. The father had been successful in a managerial position before resigning to seclude himself, his working-class wife, and their two classless and disoriented children at the Place, the great house that hovers over the novel like the House of Usher.

But the novel is mainly a sort of Gothic treatment of homosexuality, incest, and other aberrant sexual behavior. There is much vivid writing in the book, but it fails for a number of reasons: the homosexuality is artlessly handled; the symbolism is murky; and the reader is often confused by the strangeness of the people and events. Storey seems to be gradually moving away from the provincial and social novel, but *Radcliff* is not a clean break. His development will be, I think, like Iris Murdoch's—away from normal social questions and toward personal, symbolic treatments of human psychological problems.

This brief review of that peculiarly post-war novel that John Braine has called in a lecture the "new wave" indicates that the subjects which the younger writers of the British novel have chosen are quite different from those of their predecessors. Indeed, the profound social changes in post-war Britain have produced new attitudes, as well as a new group of lower-middle-class and working-class writers. John Braine's place in the new fiction is more clearly understood when his work is seen in relation to that of his contemporaries.

CHAPTER 2

Six Sketches

THE reputation of John Braine has been achieved as a writer of novels; his apprenticeship as a writer of short fiction was so brief as to be almost negligible. Between 1950 and 1957—the date of publication of *Room at the Top*—Braine wrote six sketches which appeared in *The New Statesman*. These very short pieces constitute the whole of his non-novel output except for some television reviewing for *The Spectator* in 1958 and a few autobiographical articles published after he became successful as a novelist.

It is interesting to see the contrast Braine's sketches make to his later novels, for it is amazing that the author of these undistinguished pieces could have written so powerful a first novel as *Room at the Top*. But these short sketches indicate some of the fictional techniques and characteristics later employed in the novels: they show that Braine's strength lies in local-color descriptions and in capturing the atmosphere of place in fiction. It is evident also from the sketches that Braine had much to learn about dialogue and character delineation.

I   *"Something for Everyone"*

Braine's first published work, "Something for Everyone," was a sketch in *The New Statesman* (July 15, 1950)[1] of a town hall somewhere in the provinces; and the narrator is an unidentified observer of a number of events that, somewhat to his surprise, daily take place under the roof of the municipal building. The point of the sketch, as the title implies, is that there is "something for everyone" in the government building.

The first description is of the municipal restaurant which is just across the hall from the Assize Court. The narrator, with others, is standing in line for the restaurant when he sees a woman whose son has just been sentenced to seven years at hard labor. He reflects (toward the end of the piece) that both lives will be ruined by the sentence—her respectability will now be destroyed. The clichés that summarize her life will change—

"poor but honest would become *can't hold my head up any more . . ."* (65). The narrator notes that the whole building is like a scene from Franz Kafka, and then he speculates: "Perhaps she'd only gone to the Town Hall for lunch or a dance ticket, but she'd turned to the left instead of the right, and gone upstairs instead of downstairs, and her son had been sent to prison not for robbery with violence but as a punishment for her losing her way" (65).

The next week the narrator attends a murder trial—"I used the Municipal Restaurant entrance and turned left instead of right . . ." (65). There, sitting in the students' gallery with some policemen and policewomen who are learning about trial procedure, the narrator reflects again upon the dreamlike quality of the court. The murderer, who sits with his head and hands hanging, is apparently not at all connected with the trial: "He was waiting to die . . . and there was nothing else that anyone could do for him except to kill him" (65). The evidence against the murderer is clear and damning, but it does not sound real to the narrator. The murders "might have been details of the religious rites of some savage tribe, footnotes in *The Golden Bough*" (65).

The tone of the story is fantastic—Kafka-like. The Municipal Hall is a microcosm in that everything, absurd or not, is found under its roof. We can see "a symphony concert, a boxing match, a political meeting, a dance, a demonstration of hypnotism— there was something for everyone" (65). The fantasy of the whole place, the narrator thinks, is no greater than that of Europe's recent past—"women starving amidst the rubble of their homes because they'd put a cross opposite the wrong name in 1932, families driven into exile because they'd been born in the wrong place, men tortured and hanged for one foolish word" (65).

The story, although Braine's first published piece, has a clear and pleasant style, as the quotations have perhaps indicated. The two thousand words of the sketch are chiefly descriptive, and details of the town hall are especially well done: "It was like most municipal restaurants. It was clean and well ventilated, but as soon as I got inside I never felt quite clean, I felt grubby and sweaty and vaguely unwell. It was well-organized enough; no one was ever left without a seat. But I always felt rushed and nervy and harried, balancing my tray precariously whilst steering past the crowded tables" (65). But the sketch can best be de-

scribed as promising; while not badly done, it shows that Braine
is able to organize his material and is readable.

II *"Irish Quarter"*

"Irish Quarter"—Braine's second sketch in *The New Statesman*, published more than a year after the first[2]—is a good piece
of writing. It foreshadows his fourth novel, *The Jealous God*,
which is also set in the Irish quarter of a small provincial town.
The reader smells, tastes, and above all *sees* Irish-Catholic England. Most of this twenty-five hundred word sketch consists of
tales told to the narrator, again unidentified, by an aged grandmother whose Irish prejudices were instilled in him when he was
a small child. To be English was to be extravagant, mean, glut-
tonous, vulgar, unimaginative, prudish, cold, lecherous, and
empty headed. But drinking, gambling, and quarreling were the
Irish curses; and they "were worse than all the English vices
put together, for they'd put Ireland in England's power" (124).

The grandmother told the narrator stories of the great famine,
the Black and Tans, the Fenians, and the emigration from Ireland. Her theme was the perfidy of the English, but she always
cautioned her grandson not to judge all the English by the Black
and Tans: "The best thing to do, she said, was to live decently,
work hard, and to treat them just as if they were Christians"
(124). After the narrator remembers and retells these tales, he
tells something about the woman herself and her typical Irish-
Catholic attitudes. The grandmother always voted Labour because "she thought that for the poor to vote Tory was to kiss
the foot that kicked them" (125). She disliked the wealthy—especially wealthy Irishmen, businessmen, and all entertainers except John McCormack ("who could sing even better than my
uncle Willie and who was a good decent man who stuck to the
Faith") and Bing Crosby. Crosby couldn't sing, she thought, but
"he was a Catholic"; and he had "the same wife as he'd begun
with, and four children" (124).

The narrator tells that the old woman had descended from the
first Irish immigrants to the Irish Quarter of provincial Blackersford, and for him she *was* the "Irish Quarter." She died before
World War II, and therefore she never lived to watch the decline of family life in the quarter or to see it inhabited by "Poles,
Italians, Letts, Yugoslavians, Lithuanians, Germans, Ukrainians—
from countries which would make the Ireland of Captain Boy-
cott and even the Black-and-Tans seem like Utopia" (125). The

next immigrants were workers who brought no old people with
them. The new "Irish Quarter" has become a place that wants
no old women because they make no contribution; for all grandmother had had to give was "wisdom and kindness and love."
But in the new world "no one exists unless they are useful to
the State" (125).

This quotation perhaps summarizes the theme of the story.
The young man learns much of what he knows of the world from
a limited, provincial old grandmother; however, the lessons he
learns are the most valuable of his life. She didn't live to see the
post-war world, but her general statements apply to it. Bad men
do not believe in God and do bad things, and "war always turned
people bad and cruel too; I didn't believe her. It was too simple.
Now I know that she was right" (125).

In this second sketch, quite an improvement over the first, the
old woman almost comes to life; in fact, she is almost as well
drawn as the grandmother in *The Jealous God*—both perhaps
drawn from one of Braine's grandmothers. The style is also quite
good: the short and hard-hitting sentences carry the irony, humor,
and truth of the old woman's beliefs. The descriptions of the
Irish quarter are as good as those Braine was to write later in
Room at the Top:

To this day I feel more at home in the Irish Quarter than anywhere
else—the stationer's shop with comic postcards and Sacred Heart
medallions, the little off-license shops smelling of mice and cheese, the
dark church where the silence is almost violent, the pubs which seem
permanently fixed in the Victorian period. . . . alleys twisting into
darkness, empty shops with their boarded windows blind with failure,
tusslings in the patch of waste ground behind the hoardings near the
church, the night flung like mud against the light. (124)

The description is of a provincial England like that seen in the
novels. The best part of Braine's work in at least two of his
books is the provincial background, and this sketch is a very
good example of his ability to use milieu to give point to a
story.

III   *"Nowhere"*

"Nowhere," [3] a two-thousand-word sketch of a provincial roadhouse, reflects Braine's distaste for the world that Joe Lampton
inhabits. In the sketch we can see the bitterness and disapproval
that mark *Life at the Top;* in fact, a great many of the attitudes

of "Nowhere" are found in all four of Braine's novels. Braine's acute awareness of class distinction is evident in his description of the tavern. The lounge of the roadhouse caters to the middle class and discourages anyone whose salary is under a thousand pounds; however, the public bar, which is less crowded and only charges "three-pence more than in most other pubs," is for those who make less than a thousand. Both rooms of the tavern are engaged in the same traffic—the sale of alcohol, escape, and sex. In the cheaper room, the women are less chic, "have a local accent and contrive every five minutes to show most of their legs" (250). In the lounge, the women waiting to be picked up are better dressed, speak standard English, and "keep pulling their skirts down over their knees—a kind of dishonest provocation, as if to emphasize the fact they have legs" (250).

The opening of the sketch is typical of the method of Braine in his novels: the names of the cars represent the people who drive them—"post-war Jaguars, Alvices, Humbers, Rileys, Allards, and even the odd Buick or Lincoln" are parked outside. "Cowering" near them are Fiat 500's and M.G.'s and Morris 8's, like "poor relations . . ." (250). And, throughout the sketch, the use of consumer products to describe people and levels of income is very much in evidence. The parade of brand names is one of the things that reviewers of *Room at the Top* noticed most quickly, and the use of them in "Nowhere" foreshadows the two Joe Lampton novels. For instance, the people in the Lounge

wear the right kind of shirts and tweeds which come from Harris and shoes deep brown with wear and polish and suede which hasn't gone piebald. And here are the enamelled secretary types with Bond Street accents, rather like Peter Cheyney heroines, their red-faced friends on the verge of fifty—friends, not boys or gentlemen, the providers off gin-and-it and Pimm's and Moussec (later to be paid for on the back seat of the Jaguars or after yet another drink in the exclusive flat.) (250)

Not only are the products that marked *Room* and *Life at the Top* evident as devices to fix the status of people found in the roadhouse, but there is also the disapproval of loose living that marks Braine's attitude. Evident, too, is the yearning after wealth and status for which Joe Lampton was to become a symbol. We can almost say that the attitude of "Nowhere" reflects both Joe and John Braine: both are ambivalently attracted and repelled by Jaguars and Bond Street clothes.

The style of "Nowhere," published two months after "Irish Quarter," is different from that of the first two sketches. The subject matter is responsible, I think, for the stylistic change: the hardness of the style reflects the disapproval of tavern life and general dissolution. The first two pieces show an author less disapproving and less bitter than in "Nowhere," which ends with people driving away, cars roaring "out of the parking-ground— money and lust and the pride of the eye—out of nowhere into nowhere" (252).

The point of view of the sketch is third person, and the author is completely submerged. This technique is not again seen in Braine's writing until *The Jealous God*, written fourteen years later. But the other effects of the piece—bitterness, a shiny style, and reliance on products—reappear within six years in *Room at the Top*.

IV *"Number Nine Rock"*

"Number Nine Rock" appeared in the March 29, 1952, issue of *The New Statesman* under the name of John Braine[4]—his first three sketches were signed J. G. Braine. The title comes from the Blackersford slang for the place where young couples go to court. The setting of the sketch is an amusement park at Ripley Glen, approachable only by cable cars, that is a favorite place of the provincial working classes. The little park is "a willow-pattern world of Japanese Gardens, bridges, and little ponds: . . . a merry-go-round, shove-halfpenny stalls, a zoo with a half-dozen monkeys and an iridescence of canaries and budgerigars, and coconut-shy, a shooting-range, slides and swings for the children, and an elevated railway which is simply a bosun's chair travelling at a very moderate speed round some hundred feet of rail. It's a daylight fair, a gingerbread and pink ribbons fair" (370).

There are two typical couples in the amusement park's little tea room, an old married pair and two teen-age lovers. The young are seen first by the narrator (who is more or less submerged) and then by the old couple. The older couple, who contentedly drink tea, represent working-class dignity to the narrator. The young people, typical also, will grow up to be like the old people. The boy is wearing

a check jacket with plain flannels of the same colour, and thick-soled brogues—a fashion ten years out of date and worn with a morning-coat stiffness instead of casually. His girl with her neat, mousy hair and make up applied with such odd, frightened discreetness that it makes her look ten years older than she really is, wears a pink rayon dress and a beige coat, both in those strange Blackersford shades which never show dirt but never look clean. (370)

The older couple laugh when the young ones get up to go; and, when the old man tells his wife "Ah know wheer they're going," his wife replies, "Number Nine Rock." She remarks that such stuff has passed them by, but he says, "Nay, don't say that, lass," and squeezes her waist (371). The young couple go up among the courters before catching the last train back to the city. The whole scene is pictured by Braine as being preferable to the lights of town, to the "neon lights of the cinema" which advertises "other and more garish Number Nine Rocks" (371).

The somewhat sentimental sketch has a few qualities to recommend it: the style is good; the descriptions (something that Braine learned to do well in these early sketches) are realistic; and the feeling of place, of really being in provincial England, is well handled. *The Vodi*, Braine's second novel, has many of the characteristics of "Number Nine Rock."

In the April 5, 1952, issue of *The New Statesman* (405), a Mr. E. W. Hildrick in a letter attacks Braine for being one of those journalists who write patronizingly about the West Riding. He accuses them of scrambling place names, making old people seem simpletons, and portraying all the young as poor, ignorant mill workers. Hildrick would have such writers "drugged with a surfeit of Yorkshire pudding . . ." (405). Braine, writing from the sanitarium at Grassington, replies that his picture was not of the West Riding but specifically of Ripley Glen, which he found a charming place. After defending himself on numerous other points that Mr. Hildrick brought up, Braine closes by saying that he writes of people, not of types, and of provincial England in general, not just the West Riding.[5]

V "A Devil for Dancing"

"A Devil for Dancing"[6] returns to the narrator's Anglo-Irish boyhood and is a description of Aunt O'Hara, who lived with the family. In this sketch—one very much like "Irish Quarter," except that the aunt speaks for herself much more than the grandmother does—Braine presents what is almost wholly a character drawing of the widowed, lively aunt; there is no point, no explicit theme. But Braine does make greater use than before of dialogue, and the speech of the Irish aunt is rendered very well. In describing her young womanhood, she said, " 'I was well-covered then,' she said, 'with a beautiful bosom and hips on me, God forgive me for mentioning such things befor childer' " (153). Equally expressive is her comment on a review she saw in Leeds in 1934: " 'Dancing in little short drawers,' she said 'and some of them'—she lowered her voice—'standing about *in their pelts*. Shame and them could marry, for they're nothing akin' " (153). Her one trip to the movies left her disappointed; she saw *The Sheik*—" 'it wor proper daft. Nowt but a couple of silly buggers swapping slaver' " (153).

The characterization is well done and the dialogue is good, better than some that Braine was to write later in his novels. Although emphasis is on character, the descriptions of Bradford's Silsbridge Lane are good. Bradford is, of course, a real town (Braine's birthplace); and we wonder whether Mr. E. W. Hildrick's letter caused Braine, for the time, to quit making up place names. Silsbridge Street was off Westgate Street—"Westgate was civilisation and safety, but less than a hundred yards away savagery began—the gin-shops, the brothels. The murderous fights, the Fenians in hiding. No stranger, and certainly no policeman, dare take those few steps off Westgate" (153).

VI *"Portrait of a Provincial Intellectual"*

"Portrait of a Provincial Intellectual" [7]—the last sketch published more than seven months after Braine's first novel, *Room at the Top*—is about the same length as the other five published between 1950 and 1953—between two thousand and twenty-five hundred words—but it is rather different in tone and in subject matter. As the title states, this is a portrait; in third-person narration, the focus is on a provincial intellectual who is bored and tired of his life away from the capital. The sketch ends with the indication that the next time a job is offered him in London, he will take it.

Much of the sketch is concerned with the displeasure of the central figure, one that comes about because the provinces are changing from Old England to New England. The clubs he once belonged to are now defunct; the little theater that used to produce Christopher Fry, Jean Anouilh, and Jean-Paul Sartre now produces John Van Druten, Noel Coward, and Terence Rattigan; the old buildings made of local stone have given way to "another stretch of tarmac, another block of offices, always in hideously neuter, raw-coloured concrete, and he couldn't bear to look any longer" (422).

He calculates that there are twenty thousand intellectuals in his home town, but he can't find the other 19,999. So he sits in his intellectual's uniform and wishes he could leave his cozy home and go to London. His house is decorated in the best style—when he and his wife took the house, the out-dated furniture was sent away, no pictures were put on the walls, and the kitchen name became Space Three. A bull-fight poster is hung over the fireplace—"very handy for sorting out one's guests. If they were distressed by it, you knew immediately that you'd have nothing in common: he's never met an intellectual who disapproved of bull-fighting" (421). The uniform—and this sounds like some of the pretentious types in Braine's novels— is a "bright red Jaeger crew-neck sweater, brown check Viyella shirt, dark grey Terylene slacks, plain-fronted brown suede shoes" (422).

The sketch is interesting and well written, but it lacks substance. Although an ironic and bitter portrait of the type of Englishman that Braine scorns, the reader learns very little that he doesn't already know; and he wonders why *The New Statesman* used it as the lead piece in its "Autumn Books Supplement." The sketch has none of the life of the Irish sketches, but the style is good, and the handling of consumer products is skillful— perhaps as well handled as in the novels.

Braine's other pieces, mainly autobiographical, were published in magazines; but the six sketches in *The New Statesman* are his only short fiction. Although there is nothing remarkable about the short pieces, we can see in them the shaping not only of his style but of his general fictional methods. The two Irish stories, the best of the early sketches, have a spark of life and are interesting because they give brief glimpses of Irish-Catholic life as it was lived in the North. Also they foreshadow *The Jealous God,* which pictures the same segment of English life. One or two of the early works are marred with pretension and snobbishness, the worst flaws of *Life at the Top.* In short, while the early pieces have little merit as fiction, they clearly show the strengths and weaknesses of John Braine's fiction.

CHAPTER 3

Room at the Top

WHEN *Room at the Top* was published in England in March, 1957, the praise from reviewers was instantaneous. Along with its review, the London *Sunday Times* ran the author's picture, then an almost unheard-of practice; the *Times Literary Supplement* of April 5 said, "An extraordinary vitality pulses through *Room at the Top*." The prestigious *Times Literary Supplement* noted the novel very favorably and said that Braine's "apprehension of his hero's passion" for worldly goods "is acute and exact. . . ." The review closed by calling *Room at the Top* a "novel of bounding vitality." [1] *The Observer* reviewer found the novel "remarkably good." [2]

If British reviewers were generally enthusiastic, the American ones were even more lavish in their praise of Braine's first book. When it was published in the United States later in the year, Charles Rolo in *The Atlantic* compared Braine to Amis and Wain and said that Braine "has gifts which could carry him far—humor and vitality, an unsmutty forthrightness in handling erotic love, and a capacity to project with passionate sharpness the hungers of youth." [3] *The Nation* of December 7, 1957, compared *Room at the Top* to Theodore Dreiser's *An American Tragedy* and declared that the West Riding of Yorkshire has produced "a powerful new novelist, John Braine, and a memorable young man, Joe Lampton. . . ." [4]

Commonweal deemed Braine's "creative equipment" impressive,[5] and Whitney Balliett in an enthusiastic review in *The New Yorker* called the book a "brilliantly sustained tragi-comedy" in "the line of the great English social novels. . . ." Balliett found Joe Lampton, along with Holden Caulfield of J. D. Salinger's *The Catcher in the Rye*, one of the few appealing heroes in modern fiction. Joe's affair wth Alice is handled "with delicate and touching realism," Balliett said; and the last chapter is "a masterpiece of nightmarish horror." [6] And James Stern in the New York *Times* saw the book as a first novel of exceptional power: "There is no doubt in the reviewer's mind that every

word of praise lavished on *Room at the Top* is justified." Stern
found Joe a sympathetic human being and was impressed by the
novel's "wisdom, its humor and shrewdness"; its "eye for significant detail"; and "the economy and unaffectedness of the prose
itself. . . ." [7]

Not all the reviewers were as impressed with the novel as these
excerpts indicate, but the general agreement was that John
Braine had produced an impressive first novel. Kenneth Allsop,
in *The Angry Decade*, says that *Room at the Top* sold thirty-five
thousand copies the first year, was serialized in the *Daily Express*,
and earned the author twelve thousand pounds.[8] The praise of
the reviewers and the success enjoyed by the book are not surprising when one considers that *Room at the Top* is a novel
which epitomizes its age. Like Ernest Hemingway's *The Sun
Also Rises* and F. Scott Fitzgerald's *The Great Gatsby*, *Room at
the Top* probes deeply and tellingly into a central problem of
the times. Braine's Joe Lampton is a creation of the post-war
British welfare state. Lampton is, like Julien Sorel in Stendhal's
The Red and the Black, an ambitious young man who sees only
one way possible to elbow his way to the top. Also like Julien
Sorel, he does so at the expense of his own soul; but, unlike
Sorel, he does not quite let his better nature sidetrack him into
a human act that causes his downfall.

I *Plot*

Joe Lampton, an ex-Royal Air Force crewman of working-
class origins, studies for his accounting examination while a
prisoner of the Nazis instead of doing the noble thing—trying
to escape. At the end of the war, and at the opening of the
novel, he is seen leaving his native Dufton—"dead Dufton," Joe
calls it, with its "back-to-back houses, the outside privies, the
smoke which caught in the throat and dirtied clean linen in a
couple of hours, the sense of being always involved in a charade
upon *Hard Times*." [9] Having passed his accounting examination,
Joe has taken a municipal government job in the Yorkshire town
of Warley, in every respect a more desirable place than dead
Dufton.

Joe's change of locale allows him to make a much more fundamental change of class, for in his new surroundings he is freed
from ties of family and origin and is able to rise as high as his
will and personality can carry him. In Warley, he joins the little
theater group and becomes a leading actor; his success with the

Thespians is to be expected, for Joe is a consummate actor—in fact, the whole of his success depends upon his ability to assume the dress, deportment, and speech of the upper middle classes of Warley.

During rehearsals, Joe meets and falls in love with Alice Aisgill, the wife of a wealthy industrialist and a woman who, at thirty-four, is nine years Joe's senior. He is also attracted to Susan Brown, the nineteen-year-old daughter of Warley's leading citizen and the woman he eventually marries. His relation to the two women mirrors the moral struggle of the novel: Joe loves Alice, but he knows that in order to reach Warley's silk-stocking residential area—the Top—he must marry Susan, or someone of her class and wealth.

Even while Joe is in the midst of his affair with Alice, he is conducting his cold-blooded campaign to win Susan and all that goes with her: an Aston-Martin sports car, a three-guinea linen shirt, and a "girl with a Riviera suntan." These luxuries, Joe feels, are his rights, "a signed and sealed legacy" (30). Joe plans his attack with military precision—"I was moving into the attack, and no one had better try to stop me. General Joe Lampton, you might say, had opened hostilities" (31).

The rules of Joe's war include dumping Alice and marrying Susan, who is already pregnant by Joe and whose father, as a test "to see what he was made of," patronizingly offers Joe money if he will leave Warley. And, when Joe in anger refuses him, Brown, himself a man with a background similar to Joe's, welcomes Joe to the family, the business, and the Top. Now Joe's only remaining task is to tell Alice what he has done; when he does, she kills herself by driving her Fiat into a wall. Joe's grief at Alice's death is real and touching, but not real enough to cause him to cancel any of his plans. His drunken escapade when he learns of Alice's death is one of the best-rendered scenes in the book; and at the end of his orgy of drink and grief, when Bob and Eva Storr find him alone on the street and tell him that no one blames him for what has happened, his answer—which indicates the moral problem of the book—is "oh my God . . . that's the trouble."

Despite Joe's calculated and callous actions, he is not simply a villain; for Braine intends for us to see Joe's plight as that of the young man who can rise in no other way than by wooing the Establishment. Sir Richard Rees, in a book on George Orwell, has called England the most class-ridden, class-haunted society in the Western world. Rees says that "the nineteenth-century social hierarchy has more or less collapsed. . . . Nevertheless the class bogey stalks abroad, making hearts ache and scattering chips on shoulders." [10] Since "the class bogey stalks abroad" in *Room at the Top,* Joe Lampton, being very clearsighted, knows that, if his heart is not to ache, he must become a member of the wealthier orders. And we can only call them "the wealthier orders," for in Warley there is no upper class, only a group of wealthy, upper-middle-class people who speak standard English and have either money or a university education. Susan Brown, Jack Wales, Bob and Eva Storr, and the Aisgills represent the class which Joe must be admitted to if he is to shake the last vestiges of dead Dufton and his working-class background.

The plot of the novel is rather neatly handled in a traditional manner. Braine chooses first-person narration—the "I-as-major-character" technique—and Joe therefore relates the events from a vantage point ten years after their happening. By the time he is telling his story, he is a successful Zombie (to use his own term) and is looking back to the period when he still had a choice about his future. However, even though he marries Susan at the end of the novel, the reader is not told that until it happens. In fact, the reader does not get a preview of Joe's later life very often, and only once or twice in the novel are we reminded that Joe is speaking of events that occurred ten years before. He seems to be telling the story as it happens most of the time. Joe makes the events cover no more than about a year—from the time he came to Warley until he married Susan Brown. There are some flashbacks to Joe's years in the Royal Air Force and to his life in Dufton, but such instances are few. Most of what we are told concerns Joe's attempts to rise in Warley society.

The forces in conflict in the plot are Joe Lampton on the one hand and the Establishment of Warley on the other. Also there is the struggle between the two sides of Joe's nature, though there is never much doubt about the outcome. There is, however, a great deal of doubt about whether or not Joe will succeed in his attempts to marry Susan and be freed from his Town Council job. The vicissitudes of their courtship are chronicled throughout most of the novel, even while he is engaged in his affair with Alice, which forms a counterpoint to his courtship of Susan. The illicit affair, ironically, is used to show the human side of Joe; for Joe is actually dominated by his feelings in his love for Alice. His deliberate courtship of Susan, though, is a part of Joe's calculated plan to marry a job, a way of life, and a grade-one girl.

Braine neatly balances the two affairs in his exploration of Joe's character and dilemma.

Because of the limitations imposed by the first-person technique, almost no use is made of subplots in *Room at the Top*. Moreover, in the short space of the novel, there is little room for Joe to tell other stories; but, since Joe is mainly concerned with telling of the year of his climb toward the top, he is little occupied with affairs that do not directly affect him. Almost all of Joe's energies are directed toward telling of his relationships with Alice and with Susan, and there are only a few places in the novel that show him as much concerned about other people. He almost gets involved as a surrogate son to his landlord and his wife, but that budding subplot is dropped almost before it starts. And he is seen a few times in his relations with the other municipal employees. Finally, at the end of the book, after Alice has been killed, Joe's drunken, orgiastic attempt to forget his part in her death constitutes a subplot inserted into the main plot.

The reviewer in *Commonweal* calls this episode "the most vivid and intensely moving" part of the novel.[11] And in the opinion of the reviewer in the *Saturday Review*, the last section is a short story that rises above the rest of the novel.[12] In the episode Joe goes to a nearby town to drink himself into a stupor. There he meets Mavis, a young working-class girl of easy virtue but moving sensibilities; and he seduces her on a woodpile somewhere in an alley. Her boy friend and his companion attack Joe, but he defends himself by using Judo and escapes. The whole episode is vital and moving because Joe is almost completely natural for one of the longest stretches in the novel. Also Mavis, the working-class girl, is succinctly and poignantly rendered.

But the connection to the rest of the main plot is not well established. While a man like Joe might go so grossly astray, the section seems to have a life all its own. The ending is not a serious defect in the plotting, but it seems to be told in a different mood from the rest of the story—Joe, the narrator, appears to go outside himself when he describes the Joe Lampton who is drinking himself into a stupor. It is almost as if the final section had originally been written in third person and changed to first person when the rest of the novel was written.

Braine's choice of first person has been both condemned and praised by reviewers. The reviewer in the *Saturday Review* says that the worst error in the novel is the use of first person, for "all the gusto that might have belonged to an objective story

of shameless adventure is lost. . . ." [13] Stern in New York *Times,*
however, thinks that "the author avoids the pitfalls inherent in
the writing of all first-person fiction. . . ." [14] And, when John
Braine lectured in America in 1964, one of the points he stressed
was the rightness of his choice of the "I-as-major-character"
technique.

I must agree with Braine, for the moral dissolution of Joe
Lampton is best seen from the inside. If the novel were solely
concerned with class disintegration in the welfare state, an objective rendering of the narrative would suffice. But the novel is
mainly a question of Joe's sacrificing his soul to gain the world,
and we are most interested in the price which he had to pay.
Joe's view of his world lends salience to the theme of the novel,
for the evil effect which social climbing has on Joe interests us
most deeply.

II *Theme*

The theme of the young man trying to rise by an act of will
is not new to American fiction, but it has only recently become
one of the major themes of the contemporary British novel. But,
when it has been treated by the modern British novelist, it has
often been in a satiric vein. For instance, Anthony Powell's comic
character Widmerpool of *The Music of Time* sequence, who is a
man of will like Joe, is always seen in a comic-satiric light. Nor
is Braine's treatment of the theme like that of the "Angry Young
Men," for he sees Joe more sympathetically than Wain, Wilson,
or Amis would have. Braine treats Joe as a human being faced
with a crucial problem—whether or not to give up his soul to
gain the world. And, of course, Joe elects to give up his soul.

The fact that Braine takes a basically decent person and views
him in the light of his chilling choice lends depth to the theme
of the novel. The theme is universal in that every man must, at
some time, face the choice; but he is fortunate if the choice is
less clearly marked than Joe's. Once Joe opens his campaign to
crack the barriers of money and privilege, he must submerge his
humane self and show only his created personality to the world.
Some critics have tended to dismiss Joe as an opportunist who,
when he is not climbing, takes time out to snivel; but that reading of the theme is too obvious and easy. Joe is an opportunist
against the dictates of his conscience and is disgusted at what
he is doing; but do it he must if he is ever to be anything but a
grade-ten Zombie (Joe sees all people from one to twelve on the

basis of class and position). If he has to be some sort of Zombie, he chooses to become a class two, or class one if possible.

Braine told Kenneth Allsop how the idea for the novel came to him: "I saw a man sitting in a big shiny car. He'd driven up to the edge of some waste growth, near some houses and factories, and was sitting there looking across at them. It seemed to me that there must have been a lot that led up to that moment." [15] Starting from that point, Braine explored the theme of the novel in a naturally developing manner; and the value of the theme is enhanced because Braine explores it rather than merely manipulating it. The reader does not get the impression that Braine alters the character of Joe to fit the theme, nor does he manipulate the plot so that the successful man is either completely a victim of outside forces or a villain.

Unlike the "Angries," Braine does not make Joe seem a worse man than he is; he does not make his background excessively sordid or his life more degenerate than necessary. He is, in short, a healthy young man who sees others enjoying the good things of the world and decides to obtain them for himself. If something of his humanity is lost in the getting, so much the worse; but a man may just as easily lose his humanity by settling into his lower-middle-class niche, as many of the characters in the book do. Mr. Hoylake, Joe's immediate superior at the Town Council office, is no less a Zombie than Joe is to become; Hoylake is simply a Zombie of a lower order on a lower budget.

III *Characterization*

Naturally, the characterization of all the characters other than the narrator suffers when an author chooses first-person narration. In *Room at the Top* the only fully realized character is Joe Lampton; however, since the novel is all Joe's, it is he that the reader really needs to see fully. Next to Joe, Alice comes closest to being a fully developed character. Such characters as Susan, Mr. Brown, and Jack Wales are very sketchily drawn; and that sketchiness constitutes one of the major weaknesses of the novel.

For example, Mr. Brown is the movie version of a self-made millionaire; his typical Hollywood test scene to see what Joe is made of is a cliché. When Joe refuses the offer, much to Brown's pleasure, Brown says: "'If you had owt about you, I knew you'd damn my eyes and go ahead. If you were gutless, you'd let yourself be frightened off by a few vague threats, and everyone'd be saved a lot of bother. The point is, lad, that a man in my position can't get to know a man in your position very well. So I let you sweat it out'" (268). The whole scene with Brown reveals the weakness of Braine's minor characters.

The characterizations of Joe and Alice, however, are quite good and indicate generally the mature writer. Although Alice is never seen so fully as Joe is, the reader feels that he knows her well by the end of the book. She is thirty-four (Joe is twenty-five) and unhappily married to a well-born, successful Warley Zombie. Before her marriage to George Aisgill, she was an actress in a provincial repertory company and an artist's model. After her marriage, she is a sexually dissatisfied woman who takes out her frustration by acting with the Thespians and by having several affairs.

Alice's character, though always seen from Joe's point of view, is presented to the reader in a variety of ways. We first see her only as Joe does; later, she is allowed to speak for herself in the revealing conversations she has with Joe. Then another perspective is gained when local gossip reveals some hitherto unknown affairs. Brown, when he warns Joe of her, calls her a whore; and, when Joe protests, he says: "'I use words that fit, Joe. You weren't the first young man she's slept with. She is notorious for it. . . . there's not many likely lads haven't had a bit there. She has a pal, some ole tottie that lends her a flat . . .'" (270). Brown's denunciation is the final revelation of Alice before she kills herself.

The clearest picture of Alice comes in the scenes with Joe when she is allowed to talk, for then her no-nonsense attitude about love and her openness come through. A much more honest person than Joe, she reveals her affairs with Jack Wales when Joe is talking to her for the last time. Joe at that point has sold himself to Brown, and he is accusing Alice of having loved Jack Wales (whose position in the Warley Establishment makes him Joe's natural enemy). Joe says to the reader that he would have taken Alice back if she had denied the accusation; Alice, who senses his feeling, refuses to compromise her honesty—"'I went with him twice. Once in his car, if you really want to torture yourself, and once here. He took me home from the Thespian Ball the first time.'" When Joe asks about the second time; she answers:

"That was after we quarrelled. The night after. I ran across him in a hotel bar."
"Why didn't you tell me?"

"It didn't seem important. I never asked you about your past—or your present, for that matter." (274-75)

Alice understands Joe much better than he understands her. After their idyllic weekend in Dorset, she sees that Joe will never marry her despite his protestations to the contrary. Ugly with weeping, she asks Joe whether or not he wants her to divorce her husband:

"I swear it." I looked straight into her eyes. "I do love you, Alice. I'll love you till the day I die. You're my wife now. There'll never be anyone else. I'll be with you every inch of the journey."
"There's nothing more I can say to you, Joe." She started to make up her face briskly and expertly. (236)

She knows, or senses, that Joe is lying to her and will eventually be her murderer; but she also knows that she must seize the moments of happiness before Joe sells his soul.

One weakness in the characterization of Alice lies in Braine's (and Joe's) feeling about her age. G. S. Frazer, in reviewing the novel in *The New Statesman,* expresses what any mature reader feels: "I find it unnerving, in novels by young men, to have *la femme de trente ans* evoked, always, in a tone of compassionate elegy, as if she were a silver birch shedding in autumn, her last stippled leaves." [16] Braine's Alice is, at thirty-four, pictured as horribly aged; indeed, the nine years separating her from Joe seem twice as great as they are. Joe often sees her as old, haggard; her breasts sag; her face is lined: "She did look terrible, every year of her age even in the darkness . . ." (212). "She looked thin and bedraggled; not unlike the thin women one sees in pictures of mine disasters, disconsolate and old and ugly against the pithead wheel" (147-48). And Alice sees herself in much the same way—"an old woman" (120), and "I'm too old to walk about in the nude . . ." (124). This emphasis on the extreme decrepitude of a thirty-four-year-old woman strikes a false note except, perhaps, in the mind of the very young. But, generally speaking, the portrayal of Alice is well developed and genuine.

Joe, as I have already indicated, is the only fully realized character in the novel. Little that the reader learns of Joe comes, therefore, from any source outside himself. Other characters' evaluations of Joe are limited, and only once does Alice tell him some home truths about his working-class attitudes. When he

goes into a rage over her having posed in the nude for an artist
some years earlier, she calls him a prude and a hypocrite and
accuses him of considering her his own "private dirty postcard":

"I can just see you in Dufton now, looking at nudes in a magazine,
drooling over them. Saying you wouldn't mind having a quick bash.
But blackguarding the girls, calling them shameless—" The word
came from her lips like a gobbit of phlegm. "Yes, look shocked. You've
used the word often enough with your boozy friends, though, haven't
you? I was damn near starvation when I transgressed your peculiar
morality. You wouldn't understand that, would you? You make a great
to-do about your humble beginnings, but you've never gone hungry."
Her eyes narrowed. "I wonder. I wonder. Probably someone else went
short for our darling Joe, the fair-haired charmer." (146)

When Alice also accuses Joe of not having tried to escape the
Nazi prison camp as Jack Wales had done, he admits that he
was "bloody well pleased" when he was captured. Her accusation about others having sacrificed and gone hungry for him hits
a sensitive nerve, for both his parents and his aunt had sacrificed
to make life moderately easy for Joe when he was still in
Dufton.

But we do not need Alice or anybody else to accuse Joe; he
does so himself. He almost always realizes that he is opportun-
istic and that his behavior is not that of the Establishment, nor
that sanctioned by working-class and middle-class morality. Joe
is always in agony over the moral choices that must be made if
he is to be a grade-two (or grade-one) Zombie. He is perfectly
aware that his humanity is slipping away from him as he becomes more and more successful at imitating the privileged
classes: "But the game was worth the candle; if I sold my independence, at least I'd get a decent price for it" (140). The
other Zombies, who don't go after the top prizes, sell their independence but for a low price. Joe's father told him when Joe
was a child that "There's some things that can be bought too
dear" (117). And Joe is always calculating the cost and profit of
his decisions.

From the little that Joe reveals about his later life, we infer
that he felt the cost had been too dear. However, the reader
has decided upon that independently of Joe's admission. Lost
with the submerging of Joe's humanity is his ability to feel normal human emotion as keenly as before. The final scene in the
book shows what is, apparently, Joe's last attempt to be a man.
He almost succeeds, but not quite; calculation still wars against

naturalness. After Alice's death, his grief is so great that he temporarily drops his Warley-industrial pose and gets drunk; however, he is careful to go to a nearby town where he will not be recognized. And later, when Joe is involved with Mavis' boy friends, he realizes the disaster of being caught by the police—the disastrous effect it will have on his career.

Earlier, after he has renounced Alice but before he has learned that she is dead, he sees Joe Lampton clearly and discusses him as if he were another person:

I didn't like Joe Lampton. He was a sensible young accountant with a neatly pressed blue suit and a stiff white collar. He always said and did the correct thing and never embarrassed anyone with an unseemly display of emotion. Why, he even made a roll in the hay with a pretty little teen-ager [Susan] pay dividends. I hated Joe Lampton, but he looked and sounded very sure of himself sitting at my desk in my skin; he'd come to stay, this was no flying visit. (280)

And Joe has come to stay; even the harsh truth of the cost to his manhood does not deter him. Agonize as he does over the cost, he is never deterred. At the very end, when he realizes that he has murdered Alice, he cries out that the trouble is that nobody blames him—the whole world conspires to make men sell their humanity; but he does not contemplate giving up his hard-won success. Yet the reader is made to feel a kinship with Joe, for he is not completely dead spiritually; as one reviewer said, there is still enough humanity left in him for us to cherish him.[17] That humanity is gone by the time of *Life at the Top*, and in that novel the reader is no longer able to identify with Joe.

IV *Setting*

The characterization of Joe is one of the two strong points of the novel. The other is the sociological rendering of post-war, welfare-state England and the effect that the "brave new world" has on certain people. Most modern British novelists treat the same general theme; for instance, both C. P. Snow and Anthony Powell are concerned with the same world, but their outlooks are different and their men of a different sort. The "Angries," too, treat the welfare-state problem, but their men also are different—they are the exaggerated Lucky Jims and Larry Vincents who snivel or posture before the onslaught of society. Braine's portrait of the era, while different from the others I have men-

tioned, is accurate; and its accuracy is responsible for the popularity of the novel. This is not to say that Snow is not equally
accurate on a different level; however, the corridors of real
power are not open to the Joe Lamptons of England.

Braine paints a careful, realistic picture of post-war Britain;
and he has been praised for his accurate descriptions of the
West Riding of Yorkshire, its industrial millionaires, its speech,
its values, and its reflection of the English dilemma after the war.
The events in the book take place immediately after the war—
probably in 1947—while there are still ration stamps and restric-
tions on goods. But luxury goods, Joe notes, are available to the
privileged members of Yorkshire society; for the war profits of
the wealthy can "shove by justice" and buy the good things that
are slowly being released into the market. Joe marvels at the
food on the table at Sally Carstairs' birthday party, but he reflects that her father is "in the business." Joe recalls (looking
backward from 1957) that 1947 was a time of rationing and that
one was always hungry: "Not hungry in the way I'd been in
Stalag 1000, but hungry for profusion, hungry for more than
enough, hungry for cream and pineapples and roast pork and
chocolate" (161). Joe sees the Yorkshire millionaires driving the
first post-war cars, taking the first post-war vacations, and beginning to find an outlet for their war profits; and his hunger is
made even greater.

Braine's rendering of the industrial North of England, its
houses, its people, and its speech in these expansive times is also
clear and precise. The town of Warley, which Joe observes would
be a nightmare to anyone who had any understanding of architecture, is far superior to Dufton with its "back to back houses,
the outside privies, the smoke which caught in the throat and
dirtied clean linen in a couple of hours . . ." (23-24). Warley's
city hall—"a queer mixture of Gothic and Palladian, with bat-
tlements and turrets and pillars and two stone lions"—is like a
hundred others. Joe recognizes the smells of radiators, disinfect-
ant, and floor polish—"the unmistakable Government smell halfway between a teashop and a stationer's" (24).

Braine's use of physical descriptions serves to reinforce and
heighten the theme of the novel; for instance, Joe's social climb
from Dufton to Warley is clearly seen in the physical difference
between the bathrooms at Mr. Thompson's and at his aunt's
home in Dufton. In Warley

The bathroom was the sort you'd expect to find in any middle-class home—green tile, green enamel, chromium towel rails, a big mirror with toothmug and toothbrush holders, a steel cabinet, a flush-sided bath with a shower attachment, a steel cabinet and a light operated by a cord instead of a switch. . . . it was nothing except a bathroom, it had been designed as a bathroom.

The bathroom I'd used the night before I came to Warley had been adapted from a bedroom. At the time the houses in Oak Crescent were built it wasn't considered that the working classes needed baths. It was a small room with pitch-pine flooring (if you weren't careful you could pick up a nasty splinter) and brown wallpaper blotchy with splashes. Towels were kept in the cistern cupboard, which was generally full of drying undergarments. On the window sill were a razor, a stick of shaving soap, a tube of toothpaste, and a dingy mess of toothbrushes, used razor blades, face cloths, and no less than three cups with broken handles which were supposed to be used as shaving mugs but, obviously, from their encrusting of dust, never had been. (9-10)

The whole book describes the North of England with exactness; and, before the reader is through, he has the feeling of place that the American local colorists sought to give. From descriptions of the little town of Gilden, which ended "abruptly at the Ebenezer Methodist Chapel with its crammed graveyard" that stood in view of "the moors and a few sheep and curlews" (158), to the dialect of the region, the setting is painstakingly presented. Joe's Aunt Emily's speech, which is pure Yorkshire, accurately reflects that of the Northern working class: "She wor proper determined, wor your mother. Your grandma had all t'heart knocked out of her when your grandpa wor killed at t'mill" (109). And Brown's dialect, which is slightly less heavily tinged with the speech of the North, gives Joe the feeling of Brown's solid middle-class assurance: "Ah've met you at t'Town Hall, lad," Brown says, overdoing the dialect (203).

V *Style*

The whole aura of provincial England is clearly presented to us through the observant eyes of provincial Joe. There is no condescension in the presentation of the North, for Braine is not attempting to ridicule the region; instead, he is a native son honestly trying to show Yorkshire as it is. Indeed, one of the distinguishing marks of Braine's style lies in the realism of his description. No detail is too small to be mentioned, and Braine's use of brand names is comparable to Ian Fleming's in the James

Bond stories. Teddy Soames, a co-worker of Joe's, refers to his "Brylcreemed hairs" (137). Joe, who calls himself (after he has become a successful Zombie) "a brand new Cadillac in a poor industrial area" (154), recites a litany composed of shop names and brand names in Market Street in Warley: "Findlay the tailor with Daks and the Vantella shirts and the Jaeger dressing gowns, Priestly the grocer with its smell of cheese and roasting coffee, Robbins the chemist with the bottles of Lenthéric after-shave lotion and the beaver shaving brushes . . ." (251). All the talk of brand names and the cost of goods reflects Joe's personality, but it is also an integral part of Braine's style.

And Braine's style is very much American in its emphasis on crisp, clear descriptions; on names of products; and on the Americanized culture of post-war Britain with its Cadillac automobiles and Coca-Colas. James Gindin, in discussing certain post-war novelists (not Braine, however), has titled a chapter of his book "Creeping Americanism." Much of what he says about these novelists' work is applicable to Braine's work: "these writers portray a world that is also less traditionally and uniquely British, that contains elements of Hollywood, rock and roll, and the teenage consumer." [18] Perhaps the provincial setting is responsible for the Americanized style of *Room at the Top,* for the industrial provinces have been quicker to pick up American attitudes than upper-class British attitudes. Part of the failure to imitate upper-class Britain's customs lies in the reaction against the Establishment by many post-war Britons, especially in the provinces.

Braine's writing, I think, has been shaped by American books and movies and by American-oriented provincial attitudes. His writing is free of the rather lengthy, ornate sentence structure that is considered typically British by most Americans. The reflectiveness of Anthony Powell's hero Nicholas Jenkins of *The Music of Time* or the legalistic meditativeness of Snow's Lewis Eliot of *Strangers and Brothers* is missing from Braine's work. I do not mean to imply that all British writing is cumbersome and over-elaborate, but there is a tendency toward the reflective and involuted sentence that marks the writing of most writers of the English Establishment in letters. The young writers of the post-war era rejected the style of the previous generation and imitated the hard, brittle effect of Hemingway and of the Raymond Chandler detective stories. [19]

Joe Lampton's telling of his story is as brittle as Philip Marlow's ever is in Chandler's novels. Joe is always careful to fill

the reader in on the most minute details—it "was a green Aston-
Martin tourer, low-slung, with cycle-type mudguards" (28). He
is equally careful to hurry the narrative along at a breakneck
pace—partly to keep the reader's attention and partly to show
Joe's hurry to conquer the world. There is never any languishing
in descriptions of settings or people or places:

> I felt a cold excitement. This was the place where the money grew.
> A lot of rich people patronized expensive hotels and roadhouses and
> restaurants too; but you could never be really sure of their grade,
> because you needed only the price of a drink or a meal and a collar
> and tie to be admitted. The Leddersford Conservative Club, with its
> ten-guinea annual subscription plus incidentals (Put me down for a
> hundred, Tom, if the Party doesn't get it the Inland Revenue will),
> was for rich men only. Here was the place where decisions were
> taken, deals made between soup and sweet; here was the place where
> the right word or smile or gesture could transport one into a higher
> grade overnight. Here was the centre of the country I'd so long tried
> to conquer; here magic worked, here the smelly swineherd became the
> prince who wore a clean shirt every day. (259-60)

Braine's dialogue is also in keeping with the economical style
of the rest of the book. Very rarely does any character speak
for more than a line or two; the dialogue effect is like that of
Hemingway. The following passage, in which Joe is talking to
Susan, is typical of the book's conversation—

> "She sounds nice. I'd like to meet her."
> "She's dead."
> "I'm sorry. Poor Joe—" She put her hand on mine very quickly,
> then withdrew it.
> "Don't be sorry. I like talking about her. I don't mean that I don't
> miss her—and my father—but I don't live in the graveyard." I was,
> I realized, quoting Mrs. Thompson. That was all right; I meant what
> I said. Why should I feel guilty about it?
> "How did it happen?"
> "A bomb. Dufton's one and only bomb. I don't even think it was
> meant to hit anything."
> "It must have been awful for you."
> "It's a long time ago." (91-92)

The style of the book, G. S. Frazer says, reflects its weakness.
Frazer calls the style "whorish *chic*" and "shiny-shoddy";[20] and,
though both terms seem harsh descriptions of the brittle, Americanized writing, they are not completely amiss. There is a kind

of chicness and shininess to Braine's style, but "whorish" and
"shoddy" convey little of the flavor of the writing. At times it
seems as if Braine were writing for the " slicks," but most of the
time the style reflects the period that Braine is trying to portray,
the late 1940's with "the bright, clean-cut functionalism, the carefully planned layout, often coping with 20,000 customers a week,
the 'prepackaging,' the 'oven-ready' meat in its papier-mâché
tray . . . the automatic, all-embracing, 'technological classlessness' of the times. . . ." [21] And Braine's glass-hard picture of
post-war Britain does come through in the "shiny-shoddy" style
of the book, for the pejorative term that Frazer uses describes
the times as well as the style.

VI *Critique*

The weakness of the novel, as Frazer and a good many other
critics have pointed out, lies in the confused picture of Joe
Lampton that exists in Braine's mind. "Braine," says Frazer, "is
not emotionally detached from Joe Lampton, but half admires
him" for doing what any other young man would do in his place.
"Nor does Braine seem to see the vacuity" of Susan Brown; he
is "as much beglamoured by her" as Joe is.[22] Braine does not
maintain a proper distance from Joe, it is true; and his failure
of artistic distance causes the reader to sympathize with Joe
when he does not deserve sympathy. After all, what Joe does
is not at all admirable, despite what he considers to be the necessity of his actions; and the author should not only know but
keep this fact in view throughout the novel. Instead, Braine
seems to be swept along in Joe's plans and adventures almost
as much as Joe is. To be blinded in one way or another by his
hero is a danger of which a novelist writing his first novel must
beware. And in *Room at the Top* the reader (at the instigation
of the writer) is led to feel more sympathy for Joe than his
character and deeds warrant.

The weaknesses of the novel are overborne, however, by the
strengths it possesses. Despite the lapse in the presentation of
Joe Lampton, there is never any lapse in revealing post-war
England's rapid change in values; Braine catches the tone of the
times and renders it steadily. Never once does the reader forget
that he is in a chromium-plated, teeming, industrial North Britain; nor is he allowed to lose sight of the fact that in these fast-
moving times virtue must beg the pardon of vice. The reviewer
in *Commonweal* says that the ultimate value of the novel

"will be as another sociological case history of postwar welfare stateism." [23]

The main strength of *Room at the Top* is the revelation of business-oriented and business-dominated provincial society and the dilemma it causes for men like Joe. And there can be no question that *Room at the Top* is a novel of some worth; in fact, on the basis of this first novel Braine is considered to be one of the most promising of the post-war novelists. That his later books never enjoyed the popularity and prestige of *Room at the Top* should not cause it to be dismissed as another example of slick sub-literature that deceived the popular reviewers into overrating it.

CHAPTER 4

The Vodi

(From the Hand of the Hunter)

PUBLISHED in America in 1960 under the title *From the Hand of the Hunter, The Vodi* departs completely from the theme of *Room at the Top*. While Braine's first novel was concerned with success, his second is devoted to the study of failure. And Dick Corvey, the central figure of *The Vodi*, is almost wholly the antithesis of Joe Lampton. Joe is a determined man of will obsessed by success, but Corvey spends his days and nights lamenting and excusing his failure.

I Plot

The main plot of the novel centers around Dick Corvey, a patient in a tuberculosis sanitarium, who, at the start of the novel, is considered by the hospital staff to be a terminal case. He picks up hints from nurses and patients that he is dying; and, having lost any desire to live, he considers himself as good as dead. In a series of flashbacks, the reader sees the series of failures that have caused him to lose any desire to live. Discounting any personal failure, Corvey concludes that fate has chosen to harry him to death for no apparent reason.

Corvey sees fate as personified in a group of evil creatures whom he and Tom Coverack had created in their childhood to explain the inexplicable. These evil creatures (the Vodi), who are presided over by a troll-queen Nelly, arbitrarily choose victims and, after tormenting them, kill them or make them slaves of the Vodi. Those people in Silbridge (Dick's home town) who go insane, who lose their fortunes, or who are accidentally killed or injured are always assumed to be victims of Nelly and her band. The whole concept, a harmless bit of childhood fantasy, had been scornfully rejected by Tom in his late adolescence; Dick, too, had ceased thinking of the Vodi until stricken with tuberculosis and rejected by his girl friend, Lois.

Lying near death in a sanitarium in Nedham, Dick revives Nelly and her folk and even goes so far as to tell Nurse Mallaton, with whom he has fallen in love, about them. At the nadir of his discouragement, Corvey blames his troubles on Nelly rather than on his own lack of care for his health and of success in life. Evelyn Mallaton's pity, which develops into a kind of love, helps Dick to realize that the Vodi are not responsible and that he has, through his own weakness and obsession with failure, lost the will to live. As his desire to live is regenerated by his love for Evelyn, the Vodi again fade from his mind; and, in the last half of the book, he rarely alludes to them.

After Dick regains his hold on life, he sets out to overcome the failures of his earlier years and to persuade Evelyn to marry him. His therapy is in many ways bound up with his relationship to Evelyn Mallaton; and, when she decides to leave the hospital and become engaged to Harry Thirleton, Dick almost loses himself to failure again. He even decides to remain in Nedham and become an attendant at the sanitarium instead of going out to face the non-tubercular world which had once before defeated him.

On a weekend visit to his father, who, like Dick, has had blows struck against his confidence by the death of his wife and the decline of his business, Dick makes the decision to leave the secure confines of the sanitarium and re-enter the "outside world." The two of them will attempt to rehabilitate the once-successful Corvey candy store, as well as their own lives. Dick even plans to enter the struggle to regain Evelyn Mallaton. The book ends, not altogether believably, on a note of limited optimism.

Although the story of Dick Corvey is central, the focus shifts to Evelyn for about a quarter of the book. She is faced with a choice similar to Joe Lampton's in *Room at the Top:* she must either follow her heart and tie herself to Dick Corvey with all his obvious limitations, or marry Harry Thirleton, who is successful but also somewhat crass and vulgar in an upper-middle-class way. One choice is the way of emotion; the other, comfort; and she is aware, like Joe Lampton, that financial success and security are important. However, the reader is not so sure of her wrong choice as he is of Joe's, for the Dick Corvey she rejects is not much of an improvement over Harry. She is disgusted with herself at the choice she makes, but she feels that life is passing her by and regards her attachment to Dick as the

usual nurse-patient romance that her roommate Betty Fendigo
is willing to have with Dick.

Generally, the plot of the novel is loosely knit and lacks effec-
tiveness. The series of flashbacks and the shifts in focus tend
to diffuse any possible intensity that the narrative might have
achieved. Specifically, each flashback directs the reader's attention away from Dick's present plight instead of counterpointing
it as the author intended. Some of the early flashbacks, which
are mainly devoted to tales of the Vodi and to recollections of
Tom's and Dick's adolescence, are well handled and add to the
plot and theme. But a few early ones and most of the later ones
lead nowhere and are pointless in terms of the whole plot.
There are six shifts in point of view from Dick to Evelyn, and
the flashback to some point in Dick's earlier life is employed
fifteen times.

The Evelyn Mallaton episodes also clutter and confuse the
novel, for they detract from Dick's story; and there is hardly
space in the novel for two full-scale plots. When Evelyn first
starts to become attached to Dick, the shifts to her point of
view show her ambivalent attitude toward him and are closely
related to Dick's problems. But, as the novel progresses, she
finds herself getting more and more involved with Harry; and
the reader loses sight of her continued interest in Dick while ob-
serving her moral struggles with herself over Harry. The same
criticism applies, therefore, not only to the shifts in focus but to
the flashbacks: at first they aid the plot, but their overuse de-
tracts from and fragments it. The Evelyn-Harry subplot is interesting, but its relation to the main plot is tenuous.

The fragmentary nature of the plot is made most evident when
the Vodi are dropped midway through the novel. While Dick is
very ill, the reader is convinced that the Vodi are responsible
and that he is a victim of their haphazard malevolence. But,
after he has fallen in love with Evelyn and is convalescing, he
ceases to think of the Vodi. Just at that point, Braine shifts the
emphasis to Dick's own personal failures, which the reader has
not fully known about before. The shift catches him unawares
and, like many things in the book, confuses him about the aim
of the novel. The Vodi, a reviewer has noted, are too convincing:
"We are left with two contradictory impressions: either that
Dick is right and that bad luck is destiny from which particular
individuals cannot escape; or that it is his own fault, and he
should have been like Tom. . . ." [1]

It is hard to tell in the novel just what the forces in conflict are. At first, Dick seems in conflict with the Vodi, and the reader is largely unaware of Dick's neglect of his health and of his failure to attempt a satisfactory life. As the emphasis of the novel shifts away from Dick, the reader's interest is again mis-directed toward Evelyn; finally, the reader sees that Corvey's love of failure is in conflict with his desire to win Evelyn, as well as to achieve financial success as Tom has done.

Braine's use of limited omniscience, especially since he shifts the focus back and forth between the two main characters, is a weakness of the novel. *Room at the Top* is told in first person, and all the pitfalls of more sophisticated narrative technique are avoided. But *The Vodi* contains the mistakes an author is likely to make in his first attempt at third-person writing; for limited omniscience is a more delicate medium than the I-as-major-character technique. If the writer is not careful, he blurs the focus by not limiting his omniscience carefully enough. Braine avoids getting into other characters' minds when he is focused on Dick, but he does not find a way to reveal Evelyn without rather crudely shifting the limited omniscience to her when he sees a need to reveal her. After the reader has firmly settled himself to seeing Corvey's view of life, he is jarringly taken away from the scene and into the mind of Evelyn. Both characters are interesting, but the increasing shifts to Evelyn are disconcerting, for they serve to blur the focus and interrupt the pace of the story.

II *Characterization*

In spite of the muddied focus of the novel, the character por-trayals are good—better, in fact, than those of *Room at the Top*. The characterization of Dick Corvey is full and believable. The reader knows more about him than he ever does about Joe Lampton; and, even though there is some confusion about the point of *The Vodi*, the character of the hero (or non-hero, as he has been called) is steadily presented. The reader feels sym-pathy for him and closeness to him, even when he is most dis-gustingly abject in the face of his adversity.

Corvey is more slowly and subtly revealed to the reader than Joe Lampton was, for one knew all about Joe from the first. Dick is presented to the reader in a variety of ways: by direct description, by allowing the reader inside his thoughts, by hav-ing him seen through the eyes of Evelyn Mallaton, and by having others discuss him. All these devices give the reader a more complete view of him than was possible in the case of Joe, who is seen only from within.

In the full presentation of Dick there are three stages—the present, when he is passing from despair into hope; the immediate post-war period, when he had returned from the war and was badly neglecting his health and his career; and the period of adolescence, when he was accustoming himself to blame everything on Nelly. His post-war activities and those of his early life are seen mostly from Dick's own point of view, which changes as he does. The present is revealed by Dick's own thoughts and actions, by allowing the reader to see him directly, and by Evelyn's perception of him. The later revelation allows the reader to better judge the meaning of the early life.

The scenes devoted to Dick's childhood and adolescence are among the most interesting and realistic in the novel. Braine has a way of depicting early adolescence that captures the spirit of that period of life. Like his contemporary, Keith Waterhouse, Braine remembers what boys thought about and talked about; and he also remembers, along with Waterhouse and J. D. Salinger, *how* they talked. Like most boys, Dick and Tom Coverack have nicknames for the masters at school and for most other adults, and their using of the names is natural despite the absurdities of them—Old Lammer (32),[2] Old Relentless Rupert (7), Spreadeagle Sara (16), Hellfire Ron (79), and John the Dastard (94). Also their own pastimes and amusements are real—they explored the house that Walter Perdwick, who was a murderer, lived in; found short cuts through Kellogg's Woods; told hair-raising stories about the Vodi's treatment of Walter Perdwick and Bobby Quedgeley and his sister; and stood around, like all adolescents, punching each other in the ribs and telling off-color stories:

He [Tom] hit Dick playfully in the ribs. "I say kid, which would you rather have—a bun on the table or a tart on the floor?"
It had rather shocked Dick at the time. "A bun on the table," he said primly.
Tom exploded into laughter, showing long white teeth. "That's the right answer," he said. "It's uncomfortable to eat from the floor." (28)

All the early flashbacks are well and unpretentiously rendered, and the two boys, Tom and Dick, come through as real characters. The portrayal up to the time of their young manhood is almost as well done.

When Tom and Dick return from the war, they spend the first year pursuing pleasure with carefree abandon. Dick has his old job back at Larton's, a radio and electronics firm, and his father's shop has cigarettes that he can trade for gas: ". . . there was always enough to drink because they always had enough gas to discover pubs which hadn't run dry. Together he and Tom toured the whole of the West Riding that year—it was a good year to remember, a confused but happy succession of pubs and dance halls and racetracks and cinemas and theatres" (93).

The times are flush and happy, and Dick assumes that they always will be, but Tom begins to worry and plan for the future. He decides to go into the toy business, and for several years he suffers privation and anxiety while trying to secure his future. Dick is glad to make the same gay round of parties and pubs while the others are looking toward the future. His boyhood friend Liphook, who lost a leg early in the war, spent the rest of the war years moving up the organizational chart at Larton's. By the time of Dick's return, Liphook is a senior administrative assistant and is a replica of Joe Lampton: "He still used hair oil but didn't have dandruff, and his fingernails, which used to be bitten, now were, unless he was very much mistaken, manicured. And the bird's-eye worsted suit he was wearing couldn't have cost him less than twenty guineas" (121-22).

In the face of all the portents, Dick allows himself to waste time and neglect his health. He has several severe attacks of coughing, but he merely plans to cut down smoking. Even as the attacks grow worse, he disregards them until a severe attack hits him one January morning. He hemorrhages, slightly at first and then seriously; as his father rushes into the bathroom, Dick breaks completely: "And he let himself go, he let himself fall into his father's arms; it was unconditional surrender, he'd stopped fighting, the nerve was broken, the sword snapped across the knees" (175). From this time on, the decline is swift.

The scenes that best reveal the character of Dick Corvey are those that summon up his remembrance of the past. The present Dick is a believable and natural enough character, but the rendering of the past scenes and the drawing of the characters he associated with earlier in life are the best parts of the novel. Corvey suffers, in the later parts of the novel, in comparison with Evelyn Mallaton, who shares the last quarter of the novel almost equally with him. The reader's interest shifts to her when

Dick begins to recover, and it remains with her until she leaves the hospital just before the end of the book.

Despite the rather crude shifting needed to reveal Evelyn to the reader, her character is fully realized. She is an interesting person, and her own subplot is almost as interesting as the main one of the novel. She sees herself, early in the novel, as a woman about to lose the bloom of youth, and she fears that she will become an old maid. Her devotion to nursing and her desires to help patients have caused her to come to Nedham, where there are few available men to be met. Her only male friend is Harry Thirleton, whom she describes as the "pipe-smoking Jack Hawkins type" with a "heavy chin and big nose and hard pale eyes" (185). Harry is much less interested in matrimony than he is in seducing Evelyn, and she is on the point, at least once, of giving in to his advances. On that occasion she stops him at the last minute when she reflects that he sees her as "the nurse I am going around with, wonderful little bit of stuff once she's warmed up. Cost me four quid for her dinner at the Raynton, but it was worth every penny . . ." (189).

Angered, Harry takes her home, and it is necessary for her to send him a birthday card some months later before he calls her again. This time she finds that her resistance has paid off, for he is more interested in her as a person than as a mistress. She later meets and is approved of by his mother, and on the same day Harry offers her an engagement ring, which she accepts. After that she drops from the novel except as she is remembered and discussed by Dick. Her acceptance of Harry has not been easy, for she is much more emotionally involved with Dick than with Harry. The more she sees of Harry, the more insistent Dick Corvey becomes, even to sending her letters almost daily after she is transferred from his ward to the women's section of the sanitarium.

One of his letters, along with his visit to her one day, causes her to start him a letter beginning "My dearest" and saying "I want you so much, more than I've ever wanted any man" (235). She abandons the letter, as well as her desire for Corvey, when Betty Fendigo comes in looking "too much the nurse off-duty. A sense of futility drifted into the room . . ." (235), and Evelyn sees the picture of what she is likely to become if she marries Dick. She will be his nurse, his crutch, his companion in failure. She realizes that she is hanging onto him even though she can't bring herself to marry him. She doesn't want Betty to love him; and, when Betty calls her a dog in the manger, she says, "Your genders are wrong," and then she thinks: "Neither Nurse Fendigo nor any other woman was welcome to Dick. She simply didn't want him to touch anyone else. But marriage with him was impossible; he was already married to someone else, he was a bridegroom of Nelly. From whom, as he'd said to her himself, there was no divorce. She couldn't and wouldn't marry him; but she didn't want anyone else to have him" (237).

She is right that he is, at the time, married to Nelly; that is, he is devoted and wedded to failure. But, at the end, when he casts Nelly aside and resolves to try life again, to try for Evelyn again, perhaps she will decide to break her engagement to Harry. But the ending is unresolved, and the reader is free to think whatever he wishes. Nevertheless, Evelyn does decide, while Dick is still obsessed with failure, to choose Harry's world: "the uncomplicated world in which men didn't go to bed at eight o'clock, the world in which men worked for a living and didn't have their temperatures taken twice a day. . . . she suddenly realized what she must do. It was so simple; why hadn't she seen it before? It was like the story of the man who was in prison for twenty years and who one day tried the door, found it unlocked, and went out" (238).

When Evelyn unlocks the door, she frees herself from Dick's world of failure and darkness, or so it seems to her. How much Evelyn is to be blamed for her rejection of Dick is hard to say. One reviewer compares her to Joe Lampton, marrying for money and hating "herself for the attachment." [3] And while she is, like Joe, faced with a hard moral choice, she is not so guilty of total submergence of her real self. Her feeling for Harry is moderately real, and her future with Dick would have been unspeakably bad if she had chosen him while he was still a "bridegroom of Nelly." Neither she nor Dick would have profited from the attachment, and her rejection of him can be read as her sacrifice for his sake, as well as a choice in favor of a more "uncomplicated" world.

The New Statesman reviewer calls Evelyn a concoction out of a woman's magazine.[4] While her language is trite, woman's magazine stuff—"Harry, I'm becoming rather bored. If you don't take me home this moment, I'll walk home" (243)—she has a dimension not usually found in characters in such fiction. Braine's superficial picture of her, her language, her involvement with things—her Harris tweed coat, her French Fern talcum—makes her seem to be a cheap vulgarian. And she is, coming from the working classes, somewhat coarse and vulgar, by middle-class standards. The awkward observation she makes about her fading

youth at the beginning of the book is more indicative of the
working girl than of the middle-class young woman. She leaves
her bath and looks in the mirror—"B cup and fast approaching
C if she didn't cut down on the starches, and very soon a girdle
wouldn't be something to hold her stockings up but her belly
in . . ." (178).

But her very vulgarity, her preoccupation with getting settled
before her looks are gone, and her working-class observations
are all subtle parts of the characterization. The woman's magazines and the working-class concern with settling down with a
husband are the forces that had shaped her life; it would be less
than accurate for Braine to have her talk and think another way.
And there is still another dimension to her character in her com-
passion and love for Dick and in her human and physical choice
of Harry and a comfortable life. The Evelyn that the reader
remembers is the nurse—the kind woman who is capable of
giving her heart to a dying man; the good woman doing an
expedient and practical thing in accepting Harry; the noble
woman who sacrifices her love to keep Corvey from relying on
her always.

The minor characters of the novel are, on the whole, much
better drawn than those in *Room at the Top*. Braine's first novel
had only two characters who surpassed the crudest "type character." A number of the lesser characters of *The Vodi* achieve
what E. M. Forster calls "roundness." Tom Coverack (after he
is grown), Dick's father, and Harry Thirleton are more than card-
board figures who simply people the scene. Dick's father, the
most fully drawn of the minor characters, is almost a victim of
failure himself; for the elder Corvey lets himself go after the
emigration of his older son, his wife's death, and Dick's illness.
After Dick's confinement to the hospital, the sweet-shop suffers;
for everyone is afraid of catching tuberculosis. The town council
decides to re-zone the Corvey's neighborhood, and Dick's father
is almost on the point of going to Warley to live with his daughter and her husband. Dick, who, though he has recovered, is
resigned to remaining as a nurse at Nedham, sees that his father
"like him, had put out the white flag . . ." (267).

Mr. Corvey has taken to drinking more than is usual and considers himself old and worn out. He also sees, as Dick has done,
the futility of life. Recalling World War I when the troops were
made drunk and ordered to charge at the Somme, he bursts out—
" 'Bloody governments and bloody councils! They're all out for

themselves, Dick, they'll kill you or rob you or both, and there's
not a bloody thing you can do about it . . .'" (270).

His attitude is so similar to Dick's that the son is able to see
the unwisdom of surrendering to failure. He sees in his father
the expression that "had taken over his mother's face when the
morphine had softened the pain sufficiently to let her know there
was no hope, that she was completely defeated" (271). Dick
sees himself and convinces his father that the two of them must
face life although the odds are not in their favor.

The character of Mr. Corvey is economically and realistically
depicted. Though he is not of first concern to the novel, he is
important enough for Braine to draw fully. His language is an
accurate rendering of that of the small-town West Riding shop-
keeper. His attitudes, those of the small businessman, are in no
way dressed up to make him seem other than what he is. As
an example of Braine's handling of minor characters, he represents a substantial advance over, for example, Mr. Brown of
Room at the Top.

III *Theme*

The theme of the novel is that man must accept the responsibilities of this world if he is to live in it successfully and reap
its benefits. He cannot allow himself to accept the blows of fate
without seeking to control it and stand up to life. The theme
is not especially well handled since it is not made evident to
the reader exactly what theme is being explored until halfway
through the novel. Braine attempts to explore the theme, but, in
being careful not to preach, he allows too much to happen before
the theme begins to emerge. It is not clear until later that Dick
is a weakling as well as a victim of overwhelming events. The
Time magazine statement that Dick is a "welfare state weakling"
is inaccurate, for his weakness is personal and private. As *Time's*
review correctly points out, "in his heart he knows that his own
weakness has always been the enemy." [5] If the reader had been
allowed to see the point of the novel earlier, the theme would
have been more tellingly stated.

IV *Setting and Style*

The West Riding background and the accurate rendering of
the language make the novel come alive, for Braine's most
praised skill is his ability to depict the everyday, realistic details
of life and to give an accurate picture of North Country life.

Braine does give the texture of Yorkshire life in the 1930's,
1940's, and 1950's by giving an accurate account of products and
place names, and by exacting descriptions of the North Country.
Also the speech of the characters "rings as true as the clink of
cheap teacups. . . ." [6]
There are two kinds, at least, of dialogue accurately rendered
in Braine's works—the standard North Country speech of the
middle and lower middle classes and the dialect that survives
among working and farming classes. Dinston, the male nurse
who works at Nedham, speaks broad Yorkshire to Dick:

"What dusta want, lad?"
"I'm thirsty," Dick said. "I can't sleep."
Dinston winked at him. "Dusta fancy a bottle of ale? So do I. But
neither of us can ha' one. Lemonade's poor stuff and milk's for bairns.
How about some tea?" (65)

With the exception of Dinston, few characters actually talk in
heavy dialect, except in imitation of the lower orders. Most of
the dialogue in the novel is ordinary, provincial speech (not at
all the language of the British upper classes that many Americans automatically associate with British speech). Words such
as "clot," "tinny," "rum," "sozzled," and "dozy" are examples of
provincial slang that the boys, and some of the adults, use. The
speech of the novel generally has a brassy, local-color air about
it; but it rings true.
The style of *The Vodi* is not much different from that of *Room
at the Top*. Braine retains the short sentence and the heavy use
of dialogue that were features of his first novel. The slickness
for which some reviewers criticized *Room at the Top* is also
mentioned in connection with *The Vodi*: Braine's chief danger
is "over-facility, which, at times, degenerates into the slick car-
toon. . . ." [7]
Names and descriptions give the feel of the locale, of particular
places—the fancy Raynton Hotel dining room; towns such as
Rawminster, Dufton, Warley, and Leddersford; a radio made by
Dick's company and called the "Larton Nine-Four"; cigarettes
named "Woodbines," "Corvettes," and "State Express 555." The
careful description of dress and food also gives a realistic texture
to the book. Dick is described, just after the war, as "wearing
a clerical-gray worsted suit with hand stitched lapels and an
American nylon shirt . . ." (130). At about the same period,
"He and Lois were sitting in the bar parlor of the Black Bull

drinking beer and eating sandwiches made from Nisbauer's
sausages . . ." (158). It is not enough to mention Nisbauer's
wares by name, for Braine tells the following interesting but
structurally irrelevant story:

Nisbauer, a fat grouchy German, had been making them for some
thirty years now, scorning to recognize the existence of the Ministry
of Food; Nisbauer's sausages and black puddings and pies were, during both wars, his father said, the only eatable foodstuffs to be bought
in Silbridge and when some yobbos in 1916 broke Nisbauer's shop
window the police gave them such a clobbering that he never had
any trouble again. (158)

In such observations as the one quoted above lie both the
strength and weakness of *The Vodi*. The cluttered tangle of
reminiscences and indiscriminate use of anecdotal material cause
a confusing plot; yet the best part of the novel is its picture of
the everyday life of lower-middle-class Yorkshire.

"Like Dickens, Braine is obsessed with the bizarre surface of
the contemporary world." [8] "Fewer writers today have a firmer
sense of milieu: of places that people inhabit, of things they
handle, of roles they assume. If the novel is moving back to
realism, Mr. Braine is one of those who make the prospect
attractive." [9]

V *Critique*

Inevitably, the critics of *The Vodi* compared it to *Room at the
Top;* and most of them praised Braine for trying a new theme
instead of carrying Joe a step farther or re-writing his big success,
as he was to do in his third novel. But most reviewers saw clearly
that the things Braine did well in the first book are also responsible for the good qualities of the second. "The book succeeds,"
Richard Hoggart says, "not where it tries to be new but where
it does again what was well done in 'Room at the Top.'" [10]

Hoggart's review, incidentally, is the most perceptive one on
the book. He points out that there are several things which
Braine does well—he can suggest relationships between characters and their settings; he can show certain kinds of self-
confidence; he can handle commercial, contemporary detail
(more in Scott Fitzgerald's manner than in Arnold Bennett's);
and he can describe "some kinds of raw and direct awareness;
the verbal and intellectual pugnacity of lower-middle class lads

in their inevitable pains, a nurse sick with self-disgust at finding
herself half succumbing to a man in a car on her evening off." [11]

In summary, it is fair to say that *The Vodi* is an honest attempt
to show North Country life and to analyze the characters of two
North Country people in detail. It is partly a failure, for the pace
of the novel is interrupted by the shifts in theme and in focus;
and the handling of the flashbacks is clumsy. There are, however,
several successes; for the characters are interesting and the locale
is accurately rendered. We can only agree with Hoggart that,
despite Braine's somewhat brassy *persona,* a better novelist is
trying to get out. [12]

CHAPTER 5

Life at the Top

BY having Joe Lampton narrate *Room at the Top* from a vantage point ten years in the future, Braine left the door open for a sequel, though he had originally planned none.[1] *Life at the Top*, as the title suggests, is a book about the hollowness of the life that Joe fought for so strenuously in the first novel. Set ten years after the events in *Room at the Top*, Braine's third novel covers six months in Joe's boozy, fat, unsatisfactory life of success.

I *Plot*

At thirty-five Joe has become soft around the middle and puffy-eyed from dissipation. Though Susan has lost none of her youthful good looks, she has become more and more dissatisfied with her purposeless life and has had at least one love affair. The two Lampton children are Harry, a boy of nine, whose conception was the cause of the marriage in *Room at the Top*, and Barbara, a four year old who is especially doted upon by Joe. Harry, a child shaped by his grandmother, regards Joe as hopelessly working class and treats him with supercilious politeness.

Life at A. Z. Brown and Company is as drab as the one at home. Brown had praised Joe's drive and ingenuity when he had accepted him as a son-in-law. Now that Joe is in the family and an executive in the plant, Brown's attitude toward him is patronizing; Joe's work is merely routine drudgery, and his advice is never sought nor heeded when offered. His salary is more than adequate—forty-five hundred pounds—and he is given a company car to drive; but he remains an errand boy to be belittled whenever Brown is angry. And toward the end of the book, when Brown is planning a merger, Joe's future seems far from assured.

Joe and Susan have moved from a good house to a better one with many modern conveniences and with expensive furnishings. Brown provided most of the money for the house, but Joe paid the deposit and was able to "keep up the mortgage repayments." [2]

The house has a parquet floor in the drawing room, an oil-fired central heating system, and formica tables. The way of life, like the house, reflects the Lamptons' desire for worldly pleasure: in making morning tea, "one experimented with different blends, the latest being two of Horniman's Directors to one of Twining's Earl Grey" (9). Despite the goods which Joe has, he feels "weighed down by things, all the material possessions which had accumulated during ten years of marriage, some two thousand seven hundred pounds worth, not counting my Zephyr and Susan's Morris 1000" (15).

When Joe is sent on an important assignment to London (sending his son-in-law was against Brown's judgment, but an important client had requested Joe), he meets Jean Velfrey and almost succumbs to her attractiveness. He also meets Tiffield, an important industrialist, who offers him a position with Tiffield Products. These two things cause Joe to view his life in Warley with even greater dissatisfaction; but, when he returns to Warley, he accepts, against his real desire, a Tory seat on the Town Council. The position makes him more completely Brown's puppet and fixes him in everyone's mind as Brown's subservient son-in-law. He meets Norah Hauxley, an attractive and intelligent journalist, who is doing a story on Brown. Norah, the Alice Aisgill of this novel, makes Joe even more aware of the bitterness of his life and more desirous of changing it.

When business interests cause Joe to make a second trip to London, he returns to Warley earlier than expected and finds Susan in bed with Mark, a dissipated roué and friend of the Lamptons. It also turns out that Barbara is not his child but Mark's: Mark and Susan have been having an affair for several years. Joe gets even by starting an affair with Norah.

Along with the collapse of Joe's home life has come disenchantment with A. Z. Brown and Company. Joe's recommendations for an accounting system are disregarded, and Brown plans a merger with another company without telling Joe. Lampton then cuts all his ties at once: he votes against Brown in order to humiliate him at a Town Council meeting; then he leaves Susan to go to London to live with Norah Hauxley.

His stay in London is brief. Unable to find employment and discouraged by his and Norah's drab flat with the uncertain plumbing and cheap linoleum, Joe decides that his new life is no improvement over the old. When Mrs. Brown comes to London to tell him that his son needs him because of an emotional problem which arose at school, Joe decides to return to Warley,

to Susan and his family, and to Brown and Company. The novel
ends with Joe's newest attempt to live life at the top. Little
hope is held out that he will be more satisfied than before, but
he has decided to face his responsibilities and to attempt to love
Susan. As the book closes Joe says, "With no warning, through
no conscious effort, I was happy, happier than I had been since
childhood. It could not last, it was already evaporating as I
began to be grateful for it; but I knew it would come again"
(308).

Life at the Top, viewed from almost any angle, is a failure.
This brief summary of the plot shows that it is simply an exten-
sion of *Room at the Top* without the strength and interest of the
earlier novel. The plot is, indeed, full of flaws. For one thing,
it is not always clear what forces are in conflict. When Joe seems
at odds with an evil Tory world of class distinction and super
materialism, Brown and his family represent the Tories and Joe
is the good, sensitive man crushed by their snobbery and lack
of feeling. Yet at the end of the book, Mrs. Brown and, by her
testimony, Abe Brown are more understanding than Joe. Joe
tells Mrs. Brown that he has seen through all of them—"I don't
want anything from you, I'm sick of the whole damned lot of
you . . ." (288); but a page later he is holding his mother-in-
law's hand and being told (unconvincingly, I think) that Brown
is "a more generous person than you think" (289).

Joe also seems to be in a contest with the whole materialistic
society fostered by the Industrial Revolution, and he gives the
impression that he longs for a pastoral life and an escape from
a world of things. He often wishes to stop his car in the woods
between Leddersford, where the factory is, and Warley, where
he lives. Although it is not clear what he really longs for, the
villain of the novel at times seems to be industrialism. The ma-
chine age has made Joe less important than the Flamville computer that is at the center of one of the subplots. Still, the plot
of Joe versus the modern age is not carried to its logical conclusion.

The real forces in conflict are Joe's better nature and his worse,
but the confusion in the novel obscures the reader's view and
makes him doubt which side of Joe he is supposed to sympathize
with. Braine seems to feel that Joe is dehumanized because he
did not accept responsibility, but the specific responsibility is
never clear. Joe does not understand himself, Granville Hicks
says; and, if Braine has any deeper insight, he has not been able
to show it to the reader.[3] There is a gap, therefore, between

what *Life at the Top* says and what the author wants the reader to see.[4]

Not only is the conflict of the plot obscure, the handling of the action is clumsy and there are subplots that do not fit into the main plot. Scenes are dragged in forcibly, and characters are created to complicate the plot and to solve difficulties. Jean Velfrey, for instance, almost becomes Joe's mistress on his first trip to London; then she disappears from the story completely. Apparently she is a puppet figure used in a party scene designed merely to show Joe's dissatisfaction with his "getting-and-spend-ing" existence. Totally unreal (for that matter, so is Susan), Jean is purely a vehicle for showing Lampton's growing disen-chantment with Warley life.

Tiffield, the industrialist, is an interesting minor character dragged in to offer Joe a job and to show the onerous nature of Joe's business entertaining. In the restaurant scene with Tiffield, one of the best in the novel, Braine makes the most of the old industrialist's gluttony, but the effort is wasted in terms of the whole plot. Although Braine can capably describe a business luncheon, the problems which arise in the accounting depart-ment of Brown and Company over the Flamville computer, as well as the jockeying for position inside the firm, are foreign to Braine. It is not necessary that he pinpoint the inner-factory strife carefully, but the author tries to do so and fails to convince the reader of its reality. Joe's family problems have so little to do with his career problems that the reader has to accustom himself to jumping back and forth between the two. It is hard to explain Susan's adultery in terms of Joe's business life (though she tries to do so); it is as if Braine were loading Joe with every conceivable adversity and defying him to come out whole.

One final plotting violation suffices to show the incredibility of the story. At the end of the book, Braine borrows a device from Hollywood and has the Lampton family reunited by a sick child. Harry is not physically ill, but some of his schoolmates have tried to paint his genitals in an initiation ceremony and he leaves school. For the first time in his life he needed (to use a movie term) his father. Until the end of the story, Harry has been a little stiff-upper-lip Englishman whom Joe describes as having a "sahib" attitude. At the crisis in Harry's life, the only person he can confide in is Joe. Thus Harry leads Joe back to his family to make a new and more responsible attempt at living.

II *Characterization*

The disastrous plot is not the only defect of the book, for characterizations are also weak. Braine's first two novels gave promise that the author could learn to handle characters believably. Joe and Alice were competently drawn in *Room at the Top*, and Braine showed deftness in *The Vodi* with his minor characters and some maturity in seeing inside his two main figures. But in *Life at the Top*, there is not a single life-like character presented, minor or major.

The characterization of Joe in *Room at the Top* was more than adequate. He was a real representation of the tough, self-willed member of the new meritocracy. But in the sequel, the author simply moved him forward in time ten years and eliminated the toughness and the life. Joe is dead in *Life at the Top;* and, because of his lifelessness, the reader has little interest in what happens to him. The word "Zombie" was used again and again in *Room at the Top;* perhaps it is significant that the word is never used in this novel, where the narrator is, in truth, a Zombie. Joe was moving toward death-in-life in the first novel, and the reader's seeing him take the inevitable steps gave immediacy to the story. Now that the Successful Zombie has arrived, the interest in him is considerably diminished.

E. M. Forster says that a round character surprises "because of his complexity" [5] but that a flat character has less life about him and is therefore more predictable in his responses to given situations. Joe can always be counted on to decry his lot in life and then go back for more; Susan always goes from rage to lust to tears; and Brown rumbles and erupts into provincial Toryism. There are no surprises and little complexity about the characters in the novel. There was just enough roundness about Joe in the earlier novel to interest the reader in him; but in *Life at the Top* he is completely flat and lifeless. Therefore, since the theme of the novel is serious and since the reader can't take him seriously any more, the book is a failure. To quote Forster, "It is only round people who are fit to perform tragically for any length of time and can move us to any feelings except humor and appropriateness." [6] While Joe is perhaps satisfactory in his role of a dissipated businessman, he cannot sustain serious interest throughout the whole novel.

Braine's two most fantastic creations are the Lampton children, for two more stereotyped characters would defy the imagination. Barbara's baby talk—"You're lovely warm, Daddy. You're a giant warm" (1)—imitates the speech saccharine grownups impose on some children. Harry's sophisticated responses at the first of the novel are out of character with his later behavior. He says, when told to go wash up, that he must "resign" himself to waiting for the bathroom to be free. When Joe tells him to hurry and wash, "Harry shrugged his shoulders. It was a strangely adult gesture, and typical of him; he meant, without actually saying so, that whatever I did or said wasn't of the least importance" (17).

At the end of the book, however, he cries and behaves in the bewildered-little-boy manner of the women's magazines— "Daddy, I don't have to work for grandfather do I?" and "You won't send me back there will you Daddy?" (302). The *Times Literary Supplement* reviewer justly remarked that Harry is a believable child as a "withdrawn little boy," but that his character "is totally destroyed in the first scene with his father. . . ." And Barbara, when she speaks, is "one of fiction's more embarrassing children." [7]

III *Theme*

The theme of the novel is the acceptance of responsibility, or so it seems most of the way through the book. Joe's search for goods and position has been at the expense of his soul—as in *Room at the Top*. Now, returning to his familiar characters and surroundings, Braine attempts to show just how soul-destroying his success really was. And yet the reader wonders—though Braine doesn't seem to—whether or not Joe would not have been just as fully annihilated in any life he had chosen for himself. In any case, Joe is now having to face the responsibility for causing all the sordid unpleasantness of his and Susan's life.

Life at the Top is a very moral novel. In the only favorable review of the book, Milton Rugoff speaks of the almost old-fashioned morality and calls the book "a mature novel, called on to face, like Joe himself, far larger problems than 'Room at the Top.'" [8] Although not a mature novel, it does try to confront more serious moral problems than Braine's first novel. Braine explores what causes the unsatisfactory life and, by implication, the satisfactory one. Joe should make the discovery that it is in "wanting things, not having them, that one comes at all close to happiness"; but he is incapable of clearly visualizing that concept. [9] Perhaps Braine doesn't see the sourness of success as clearly as the reader does. That moral is obviously pointed to, but "Braine destroyed it by a curiously sentimental double take, as though the author and his creation were weeping on each other's shoulders." [10] Braine's lack of clarity about the moral blunts the thematic effect of the book. The same criticism applies to theme in *The Vodi* and in *Room at the Top*, for what is clear to the reader is apparently not clear to Braine himself.

While the main theme of the book is concerned with moral responsibility, there are some lesser themes that stand out quite clearly. One of them is stated by Mrs. Brown toward the end of the book: "There's more to having children than begetting them" (286). This theme is not a new one in Western literature; for instance, it is explored in Arthur Schnitzler's play *The Lonely Way*. However, it is not one that has been much explored. Braine only suggests it in the novel, and Joe is the only character much concerned. Mark, if he knows, does not care about his father-hood of Barbara. In Schnitzler's play the "real" father kept the secret in his heart as a prop to his old age only to see it collapse when the son rejected him in favor of the man he had always assumed to be the father.

Comparing *Life at the Top* with *The Lonely Way* shows the shallowness of Braine's sub-theme: what could have raised an interesting and subtle moral issue is treated in a cursory, un-satisfactory manner. We might argue that this theme is minor to the novel and needs no further exploration, but the fact is that all the embarrassing scenes with Barbara and all the interest Joe shows her as his favorite build up to the climactic revelation that Barbara is not his daughter. Then, with very little soul searching or speculation, Joe resolves his feelings and accepts her again. The easy acceptance comes after all the emphasis upon her being *his own* child. Joe always seems to say in moments of despair, "at least, I have Barbara." Braine builds the reader up to expect more reaction in Joe than Braine gave him in the first place, and the easy resolution is a kind of artistic betrayal.

And there are other themes in the book that have promising starts but unsatisfactory conclusions. The inner struggles of the business world are talked about and described, but the reader is left with some question as to their meaning in terms of the whole novel. Also confusing is the attempt to view the Joe-Norah rela-tionship as anything but a plot device to show Joe's disenchant-ment and temporary departure from Warley. In short, the themes are suggested; and, like several of the subplots, they weaken the novel by being undeveloped or united to the other themes and the action.

IV Setting

Lacking most noticeably in *Life at the Top* are two qualities in Braine's work that heretofore were praiseworthy—the sense of place and the reality of life. The first two novels, despite other flaws, were always true to their locale; and, when Braine turned to the North Country which he sprang from, the reader could count on unfailing honesty and verisimilitude. But such is not the case in *Life at the Top;* there is no sense of seeing local life as it really exists. There are descriptions of the countryside, but they, vague and general, carry none of the immediacy of *The Vodi.* In Braine's second novel, the reader really felt himself in Kellogg's Woods or in the area around the hospital at Nedham, but now Joe's rather sentimental yearnings for that stretch of road between Leddersford and Warley only serve to reinforce the maudlin nature of the whole book: "For ten years now this drive home had been an escape; every inch nearer to Warley had been a further distance between my father-in-law and my father-in-law's world" (33).

In *Room at the Top,* Joe's continual looking around him at the goods and dress of people was always counterpointed against his working-class past. There was always a shifting between past and present that gave an actuality to the character of the tough boy from the West Riding. In *Life at the Top* Braine cuts Joe loose from the working-class moorings that held him firmly aimed at his goal and allows the whole harsh picture of the countryside in the throes of industrialism to evaporate. The evaporation of the sense of place causes the character to become as fuzzily realized as the setting. There are only one or two places in the book that take the reader back to the Joe who ached for success and who cut his ties with the past. Ironically, the incidents that capture Yorkshire life are ones in which Joe wishes to abandon his success in favor of his earlier period of growing desire.

While eating dinner with Tiffield at the Savoy on an expense account, Joe sees the "private persons" dancing and spending their own money:

This would be a big night, they'd be enjoying themselves, an evening at the Savoy would be something worth remembering. Eleven years ago, I'd gone regularly to the Dufton Locarno; there too I'd sat upstairs, and ate and drank and watched the dancers. I'd eaten sausage rolls and drunk tea or coffee and my suit had cost nearer ten guineas than thirty-five; but I had been a private person, spending my own money. And I had been free to join the dancers. (48)

It is only when Braine can have Joe "join the dancers"—be a small-town person openly yearning for life among more fortunate people—that he can draw a convincing picture of life. Braine, himself a product of a town in the West Riding, can only describe the life he has known. When he begins to chronicle life lived at the top, he fails to render the picture truly. He turns Joe from a character filled with the "buoyancy and sharp-eyed precision" of the man on the make to a "poor little *nouveau riche* boy." [11]

Several reviews remarked that much of *Life at the Top* was fantasy. Braine's conception of what is "materially smart" is naïve, and the lunch with Tiffield, the *Times Literary Supplement* reviewer said, was a flight of fantasy from start to finish.[12] Walter Allen, reviewing the book for the New York *Times,* observed that the novel lacked what *Room at the Top* had: "the sense of actuality of the community that made the first novel so exciting." [13] Another reviewer noted Braine's false notion of what constitutes life at the top. Because money is central to his concept, the legal, medical, or academic professions don't qualify for a place at Braine's top.[14] The same reviewer also pointed out the fantasy of the sex passages and says that they are not so much created as "daydreamt." [15]

V *Style*

The daydreaming—the fabricated quality that destroys theme, character, and setting—is also patently evident in the style of the novel. Braine's first two novels were alive and readable in a clear, workmanlike narrative style. Most of the time Braine was able to sustain the crispness of the writing; even when he foundered or noticeably strayed from his plot, his writing saved him. Never especially good at recording speech (despite a good ear for dialect), Braine managed to avoid being embarrassing when his characters spoke. At his best, Braine's dialogue is stilted, but in *Life at the Top* the dialogue collapses and the characters "chatter indistinguishably." [16] The following passage shows the horrible turn that dialogue can take when taste lapses:

She [Mrs. Brown] sighed. "You can't possibly have read Abe's letter."

"I didn't. I burned it."

"Oh God!" Her face seemed to elongate itself grotesquely with pain. "You hate us. You really hate us. Why, Joe, why? Why so much? There was nothing in the letter to hurt you. Abe's sorry for you. He feels a certain responsibility for what happened—"

"He ought to," I said.

"Yes, he ought to. We both ought to. But don't ask too much all at once, Joe. There's no question of your being sacked. Abe realizes you need time to think—"

"He knows too, then."

She shook her head. "There's a limit to the shocks he can stand. I don't see any need for him to know."

"Don't be frightened," I said. "He won't learn it from me." (287)

This passage, representative of the dialogue style, perhaps explains why the *Daily Express* serialized the novel; for the writing is in the popular confessional, television idiom. *Time* magazine, reviewing the movie made in 1965 of *Life at the Top,* said that the movie was "leagues away from the microcosmic Warley, Yorkshire, and a stone's throw from *Peyton Place.*" [17] Nowhere is the soap opera more evident than in the talk, talk, talk that fills the pages of this book. Moreover, the story ends in a sentimental reconciliation scene that must have delighted the book-club readers and the *Daily Express* followers of the serial. A short sample serves to show its triteness:

"It took me a long time to work it out," I said. "But she's right. Children don't choose their parents, but parents choose their children. I know you told me the truth. But I love Barbara, and I can't stop loving her now. She's my child just as much as Harry is. I've made myself her father. It's easy for you to know who your child is, but I've got to find out by loving the child. Perhaps Harry wasn't my son until tonight."

She stroked my hair. "You won't go back on what you've said, will you, Joe? You won't be bitter?"

"I won't go back on what I've said. I don't know whether I'll be bitter or not. But I'll try." (306)

The narrative style is somewhat better, but it is not distinguished. The lapses of taste are fewer in the straightforward telling of the story than in the dialogue; however, nowhere in the novel is the writing so alive, so objectively clear, as it was in the first two novels. As always, Braine uses short, hard-hitting sentences and much shorter paragraphs than most writers use. The main reason for the short sentences and paragraphs is that

given by journalists—the common reader is discouraged by
longer sentences and bored when he sees full paragraphs and
little dialogue. In fact, one of the formulas for commercial magazine stories is to start with dialogue; and the appeal of *Life at
the Top* is to the *Daily Express* sort of common reader. For
example, two inexcusable paragraphs follow Joe's finding Susan
and Mark in bed. Joe plans to rush in and attack the lovers:

> I was six feet and he was five feet seven. I was clothed and he was
> naked. I knew he was there and he thought I was two hundred miles
> away. It was almost too easy, too delightfully easy. And I wouldn't
> kill Susan either. There are worse things to do to a pretty woman
> than to kill her.
> I was on my feet and halfway up the stairs before I remembered
> Barbara. There would be a scream, at least one scream; she would
> wake up and run into her parents' bedroom, holding the panda tightly
> to her. And what she would see in her parents' bedroom would crack
> her world from side to side. That was it precisely; the mirror would
> crack, there would be no repairing it. I had her life in my hands.
> (171)

The harsh swiftness of the primer sentences and the fast-paced,
breathless sense of action are found in American detective stories
—and not in the best ones. The repetitions—"too easy, too de-
lightfully easy," "There would be a scream, at least one scream.
. . ."—give power to the brutal Mickey Spillane toughness. The
unspoken threats—"there are worse things to do to a pretty
woman than to kill her"—lend menace to the scene. Finally, the
pure soap opera of the last sentence—"I had her life in my
hands"—makes the reader shudder at Joe's cruel restraint. But
such patent dramatics will not do in serious fiction.

One facet of the style that is unchanged from the earlier novels
is the reliance on brand names to pinpoint individuals and states
of mind. In *Room at the Top,* one of the best effects Braine
achieved was in having Joe see the whole world in terms of
names for products. In *The Vodi,* the same technique served a
purpose, one also served in this novel; but I begin to wonder
how far Braine can take this technique as a substitute for more
penetrating insights. In 1947 Joe might well have seen the world
in terms of the names of things he wanted, but ten years later
Joe should have progressed somewhat—or Braine should have
in five years. Brand and trade names are an easy way out of
fuller, more mature analysis: "It is as though everything and
everyone wore a tag on which was meticulously detailed price,

horse power and performance. At times it reads less like a novel than a fictionalized consumer's report." [18]

The names of products are a kind of symbolism for Braine, and almost the only symbolism he uses. Joe does refer to himself as a "citizen of the green and buff country of watch your step keep your nose clean you can't be too careful" (84). And at the end, he and Norah refer to Warley as Capua—the Roman town where one "led a life of luxury and ease" (278). Joe tells her that he must return for a short time to see about Harry:

> "Have a nice time in Capua," she said.
> "I'll be back," I said.
> "No one ever comes back from Capua," she said. (296)

These two examples represent the scope of Braine's symbolic usage. Things are open, straight, unsubtle, and clear in *Life at the Top*. Partly this is a concession to the common reader and partly, I think, it is the way Braine sees the world. The Vodi, of course, were symbolic, but in the most elementary way; and it did not require a symbolic turn of mind to create them. It is not a pejorative criticism of a writer to say that he is not a symbolist, but dearth of symbol may reveal the nature of a writer's thought.

VI *Critique*

The book, taken all in all, is a failure. Braine made a mistake to go back to a vein that had already been worked out in his first novel. A great many authors, especially after a successful first novel and a second novel that fails, are tempted to return to the formula that appealed to readers at first, or publishers urge them to do so. *The Vodi* was a more ambitious work than either *Room at the Top* or *Life at the Top*: it was an attempt to study the mystique of failure from the viewpoint of the one who fails and of the one who is affected. The result was not what readers and critics had expected; moreover, the novel was flawed in several ways and *The Vodi*, therefore, did not succeed. Trying to recapture his audience, Braine turned next to *Life at the Top*, a book he had not planned to write. The unhappy result was a badly executed novel.

Almost to a man, the critics thought the book unsuccessful. Granville Hicks, who in July, 1962, had praised Braine and called him one of the leading young writers, withdrew Braine's name from his list of promising authors when *Life at the Top* appeared.[19] A. Alvarez, reviewing the book for *The New States-man*, called the plot a "kind of Tory fairy tale" and observed that Braine tried to make up for the failure of *The Vodi* by using the same formula that had made *Room at the Top* popular, "a heavy dose of . . . success and consumer goods."[20]

Richard Hoggart, a perceptive reviewer of Braine's novels, points out that the last third of the plot creaks with plot ma-neuvers. In the case of Norah, Braine "levers her abruptly and carelessly out of our sympathy" when he is ready to send Joe back to Warley.[21] The movement of the novel depends upon a series of events "too pat" or "too tricky" to carry conviction.[22] In a scathing review of the novel, Mordecai Richler says that "only the most naïve book-club reader will not always be at least one step and a chocolate ahead of the writer."[23] The *Times Literary Supplement* reviewer says that Braine imposed "events on characters rather than waiting for them to create their own."[24]

Only one reviewer, Milton Rugoff, writing in the New York *Herald Tribune*, had anything good to say of the novel. He found Joe more mature, the style improved, and the theme more substantial.[25] One or two critics still saw something to praise in the sprightly, workmanlike style; but most found even that objectionable. It must be admitted, I think, that the novel is an embarrassment to admirers of Braine's work.

CHAPTER 6

The Jealous God

AFTER the startling success of *Room at the Top* and the just
as surprising failure of *Life at the Top*, no critic was sur-
prised that John Braine abandoned the chromium world of Joe
Lampton in his fourth novel, *The Jealous God*. In this novel he
returns to the less spectacular, small-town Yorkshire life that he
had pictured quite well in *The Vodi*.

Admirers of Braine were relieved to find that *The Jealous God*
was not an imitation of anything he had written before but was
about a new theme set in a circle of Yorkshire life that he had
not treated before. Unlike the Joe Lampton novels, *The Jealous
God* never visits the modern industrial world of Warley with
its struggles for business and social success. And, unlike *The
Vodi*, the lower middle classes and the working classes of industrial Yorkshire are not the focus of the book. Instead, Braine
draws his characters from the Irish-Catholic middle class of the
region who came to the West Riding during the potato famine
and who comprise a social class different from any seen in his
first three novels.

Admirers of Braine's work were also relieved to find that *The
Jealous God* was a good novel that needed no apologies made
for it. Peter Buitenhuis, who had feared that Braine might be
a one-book novelist, said: "It is a pleasure to report that this is
a good novel." [1] Wilfred Sheed called it "a first-class novel," [2]
and Granville Hicks, who had previously removed Braine from
his list of "English novelists worth watching," said: "Now, after
reading *The Jealous God* . . . I have to reverse myself again." [3]
Most of the reviews, both here and in England, were good; and
most reviewers were pleased that Braine had not lost his in-
ventiveness and his ability to strike out on a new artistic tack.

I *Plot*

The Jealous God is concerned with the moral dilemma of
Vincent Dungarvan, whose mother wants him to be a priest but
whose love for women is greater than his desire to join the

clergy. Born into a tightly knit Irish-Catholic family, Vincent is
the youngest son, who at thirty is still wavering between the
desire to marry and to please his mother. Having a priest in
the family, Vincent realizes, is Catholic snobbery on his mother's
part; but he can't be sure that he doesn't have a calling to the
ministry. Vincent, as the novel opens, is still chaste; but his desire for women has almost cost him his virginity several times.
He has just gotten himself disentangled from Clare, "a nice
Catholic girl," and is again strongly considering the priesthood
when the novel opens.

Vincent's wavering between marriage and the priesthood con-
sumes a fifth of the novel, but he is becoming more and more
certain that he wishes to marry. Then he meets Laura Heycliff
and falls in love with her. First, he finds out that she is a Protestant, which is only a minor bar to his plans; next, he learns
from her roommate that Laura is divorced. Therefore, marriage
is out of the question because he finds that he is unable to cut
his ties to the church, and it forbids marriage to a divorced person. In an agony of frustration and desperation, Vincent com-
mits adultery with the slatternly wife of his brother Matthew.
Part I of the book ends with Vincent cut off from the priesthood
but denied marriage with Laura, the only woman he has wanted
to marry.

When Part II opens, Vincent is indulging his desires in an
affair with Laura. He makes no long-range plans for marrying
her, he won't cut himself off from his religion, and he can't see
any future for their happiness. He ceases going to confession,
for he would have to promise to give up the sin; he therefore
dreads the coming of Easter when he will have to go to confession and make some kind of decision. His limbo of indecision
is only settled when Laura starts living with her husband, whom
she had divorced because of his homosexuality. A further com-
plication of Vincent's problems is the fact that his sister-in-law
Maureen is pregnant with his child.

The crisis is resolved when Maureen's baby is born dead and
when Robert, Laura's husband, kills himself because he thinks
Laura is pregnant with Vincent's child (Robert had confronted
Vincent, who did nothing to discourage Robert's thinking that
Laura's child was not his own). After Robert's suicide, it turns
out that Laura is not pregnant, and she and Vincent have no
bar except her religion (that she is willing to change) standing
between them and marriage. Although the book ends the night

Laura learns of her husband's death, and although Vincent is still not married, the reader is left with the clear impression that he will marry and that his mother will approve: "When his mother came into the room he did not take his arm away from Laura's shoulder." [4]

Except for the hasty dénouement, always one of Braine's chief weaknesses as a plot technician, the structure of the novel is an advance over the other three novels. Using third-person narration for the second time—he used it in *The Vodi*—Braine keeps the focus steadily on his main character, Vincent. Where *The Vodi* was flawed by shifting focus and awkward flashbacks, *The Jealous God* progresses straight through the five or six months that constitute a time of crisis in Vincent Dungarvan's life. The limited omniscience of the narration never wavers from the central character, and little is learned about others in the story that is not revealed by Vincent or by dramatic revelation of the characters in scenes with him.

The chief structural device of the novel is the progression from one self-contained scene to another—a method that has marked Braine's novels from the start. Although there is nothing startling about a writer's moving his story forward in a series of scenes, Braine's rather short scenes are a dominant mark of his structure and influence the totality of the novel. As a result, it is easy to chart the number of distinct scenes that occur. In *The Vodi*, for instance, almost every shift in scene involved a flashback or a change in focus. In *The Jealous God*, the seventeen changes of scene in each of two parts of the novel are created as Vincent moves from one place to another. The material is carefully controlled; though the reader is not acutely aware of rapid shifts, he has the illusion of seeing a great deal happen in a short space. The two Joe Lampton novels proceed by short scenic units, and while neither book is much over three hundred pages, each imparts a sense of much having happened.

Except for the already mentioned weakness of the dénouement, the plot of *The Jealous God* is very satisfactory, primarily because the plot grows naturally out of the nature of the characters, especially the chief character. There is never any feeling, until toward the end, that there is an author behind all the activity recorded. Vincent's mother's desire to have him renounce the flesh for the priesthood, his own unsettled state of mind in regard to marriage, and the pressure first by his family and then by Laura provoke all the twistings and turnings in Vincent's life

and in the plot of the novel. These forces in conflict are rather
clearly marked early in the story, and the reader is content to
see them entangle and then unravel. Only at the end does Braine
"get his characters off" with some unnatural events.

II *Characterization*

The characters themselves are stronger and more life-like in
The Jealous God than in Braine's first three books. Vincent
Dungarvan has a complexity which is missing from Braine's other
major characters, and the novel has more successful minor characters, by far, than the other novels. Vincent surprises with his
complexity, as E. M. Forster says a round character must do; for,
just as the reader has Vincent analyzed, he makes some very
human and unexpected move.

As the novel opens, Vincent is seriously concerned about going
into the church, which is what his mother fervently wishes him
to do. The reader learns, later in the book, that Vincent has
previously made an appointment with Monsignor Carndonagh
to discuss the question of vocation. The meeting takes place
halfway through the book, and Vincent announces to the Monsignor what the reader has known for some time: he does not
have the calling. Then in a burst of candor he says: " 'I thought
that I didn't really like women, I thought that I was above sex.
I found myself attracted to a girl despite myself, then ran away
when I discovered that she was married. I should have been
happy at my escape but instead I was frustrated and savage and
I let myself be seduced by my brother's wife. Now I can get
neither her nor the other woman out of my head . . .' " (155).

This speech summarizes the plight that Vincent finds himself
in. He has wasted much of his life trying to decide whether he
has a vocation; he has kept himself chaste because of his acute
consciousness of sin and the possibility of vocation. When he
finally meets a woman whom he can love and marry, she turns
out to be unacceptable on other grounds—her Protestantism and
her divorce. Vincent's utter frustration when he learns of Laura's
marriage causes him to violate his thirty chaste years in the most
horrendous way possible. The scene in which Maureen seduces
Vincent is the most shocking in the book because it is so unexpected. Vincent is not the kind of man to give in to lust for anyone, least of all, we are convinced, for his brother's wife. And
yet, when he does, the act is believable; for the frustrations in
Vincent's life are violently intolerable. His relationship with his

mother, his family, Laura, and his soul have stretched him farther than man can stand.

Basically, Vincent is a tolerant, slow-moving man who is very
sensible of his responsibilities—the sort of man who is described
as "steady." His relationship with his mother appears to be the
classical mother-bachelor-son type, but it is in no way Oedipal.
She keeps house for him and interferes with his life as little as
possible except in regard to his marriage and his vocation. She
has always hoped that he would be a priest; failing that, she
hopes, as do all his family, that he will marry "a nice Catholic
girl." Only when he becomes involved with Laura does Mrs.
Dungarvan begin to pry into his life seriously and to scream at
him—"You're going out with that bloody Protestant woman
again, aren't you?" (130). "'He's going off to that whore. My fine
handsome son's going off to the arms of a married woman. My
pride and joy, my fine clever son who I thought one day would
even be one of God's holy priests'" (131-32).

To the rest of the family, Vincent is the favorite uncle with
the inevitable presents. He is the brother who is always good for
a loan, and he is always courteous when his brothers and sisters-
in-law tell him how to run his life. Both his brothers regard
him as sensible but as ascetic and other-worldly enough to be a
priest. As a teacher in the local Catholic grammar school, he is
respected for his learning and for his ability to manage the boys.
In short, he is the very model of the educated, sober young
Catholic layman who is expected some day to become a priest.

This façade is, however, about to shatter as the novel opens.
Vincent is sick of being dominated by his mother, his brothers,
public opinion, and the strictures of the church. And he bursts
all the bonds that have held him together for thirty years. The
break at first appears final, for he seems to cut his ties completely. The Protestant woman, the seduced sister-in-law, the
open flouting of small-town morality—all these episodes sym-
bolize his revolt. But then—and this incapacity is what makes
him a full and human character—he is unable to go the whole
way: he can revolt against his mother and his family, but he
can't submerge his awareness of sin; he can never harden his
heart to the extent of leaving the church to marry Laura; and,
despite his protestations to the contrary, he cannot live in what
the church has taught him is mortal sin.

The struggle that envelopes him after his revolt is involved
with the attempt to return to his earlier state while "retaining

the offence" that led to his break with the church. He wants
to keep Laura and his religion—an all too human desire. Re-
luctantly, he gives Laura up and finds himself more miserable
than before. His sacrifice of Laura leads him to another kind of
sin—despair—for, after one confession, he reflects: "he couldn't,
he thought, very well say that his sin was to be neither hot nor
cold, to wish neither to hurt nor to be hurt, to wish only to do
his job and, increasingly, to escape into fantasy" (278).

Vincent is saved, however, by John Braine. For the impossible
situation is resolved when Robert kills himself and clears the way
for Laura and Vincent. At the time, Vincent is planning to leave
Charbury and his family to live in Berkshire. A character in real
life might have gone quietly to Berkshire, or perhaps would
have married Laura despite her divorce. Nevertheless, the contrived ending does not destroy anything of the character that
has been presented. We are satisfied that we have seen a real
person confronted with a moral problem that to him is the most
crucial of his life. That he cannot solve it doesn't make the artistic creation any weaker, for the reader has seen the man confront sin and his conscience and do so in a plausible way.

The main character of the novel is a complex creation that
reveals Braine's stature as a novelist. At times Joe Lampton and
Dick Corvey fail to convince the reader of their humanness, but
never once does one feel that Braine is manipulating his pro-
tagonist's character or that he is creating a type. Manipulating
the plot is one thing, but perhaps Braine does that rather than
having Vincent act out of character to fit the circumstances of
the plot. It seems to me to be a high kind of artistic integrity
to remain true to the people one has created. To tamper with
the plot is an artistic flaw but not a betrayal.

Moreover, Vincent is not the only well-drawn character; indeed, there are a surprising number of very good minor characters in *The Jealous God*. Vincent's old grandmother, his mother,
and his brother Matthew are all carefully drawn, substantial
characters. The persons of the novel who are seen only once or
twice frequently take on a dimension not always found in very
minor characters. For instance, Monsignor Carndonagh, who is
seen in only one small scene, is strikingly real. He is much more
than the wise and kind headmaster type often introduced into
similar situations. He has a human worldliness that is many
times observed in the upper clergy. His administrative trick of
appearing busy when Vincent comes in, his reputation for shav-

ing three times a day, and the trite advice (given after some sensible things have been said) for Vincent to find himself "a nice Catholic girl" reveal him as someone we could meet in life. It is the device of a good novelist to concern himself with all sorts of little, apparently pointless bits that lend reality to the novel. In the early novels Braine showed a knack for careful descriptions of places and things, but his very minor characters often lacked details that could have brought them to life. In *The Jealous God* nothing minor is overlooked.

Next to Vincent, the most interesting character in the book is Mrs. Dungarvan. Her position as protector of Vincent and as matriarch to the other Dungarvans is well developed. And when Vincent meets and falls in love with Laura, Mrs. Dungarvan opens hostilities on a large scale. Her two other sons and their families become troops in her holy crusade to save Vincent; her influence is also felt in other places: Monsignor Carndonagh "just happened" to meet her before Vincent's visit to him. The more Vincent strays, the shriller and more tenacious she becomes.

Mrs. Dungarvan is one of those Catholic women who, in fiction at least, regard themselves as guardians of the church as well as recruiters of priests. When Laura asks her if she may attend the funeral of Vincent's grandmother, she replies that God's house is open to all, but Vincent thinks sourly: "It was as if St. Maurice's were her private property . . ." (250). Her role in the family is as autocratic and domineering as her role in the church: she knows what is best for all her children. When Matthew needs a loan, she reminds Vincent that he ought to offer one because Matthew is too proud to ask. When Vincent reminds her that Paul is well-off, she says: " 'Paul has three children. Paul has appearances to keep up. Paul's considering buying himself a partnership. You've only yourself to think about, and you're very careful with money. Though no doubt you weren't when you were gallivanting around with Madam Heycliff' " (158-59). No one is safe from her family spy network, or immune to her sharp tongue.

Her struggle to keep Vincent true to his church is what makes his life so miserable. In the end she wins, for her son finds that he is unable to rebel successfully against what she and the church have taught him. She is also concerned lest Vincent follow in the path of his father, who was a libertine. In fact, the father whom he admired so much lived the sordid life that Mrs.

Dungarvan is fighting to protect her son from. When Vincent
praises his father and accuses his mother of having made his life
miserable, she says: "'He died with a woman. The same woman
you cast your eyes upon one night at the Hibernian Club of all
places. In the act, in the act of adultery, in mortal sin, that's
how your fine father died. Now you know'" (270). Vincent is
greatly shocked to learn the facts of his father's death, and he
accuses his mother of having hated the father as much as
she hates him. "Hate him?" she said. "Hate him?" The tears
suddenly ran down her cheeks scoring paths through the face
powder. She did not attempt to dry them but ran her hands
through her already disheveled hair again, a middle-aged woman
ravaged by grief. "I loved him. You fool, you cold fool, I loved
him" (270).

This scene gives a dimension to the mother that neither Vincent nor the reader has been aware of. She is revealed throughout the novel as meddling, aggressive, harsh, and proud; and she
is all of those things. But, more important, she is human, more
human than Vincent in many ways. She recognizes things in
Vincent of which he is not aware, and her fear for his soul is
genuine and touching. Until this scene, she is almost a stock
character, but her outburst adds to her character and makes her
more human.

III   Setting

Another aspect of this novel that makes it rise above the ordinary is its excellent exposition of the milieu of Irish-Catholic
life in Protestant Yorkshire. Braine, a member of the class por-
trayed in *The Jealous God,* is almost always expert in making
place reveal characters and theme. But this novel surpasses *Room
at the Top* and *The Vodi* in that respect.

The life that the Irish-Catholic community in England leads
is little known in fiction, and *The Jealous God* portrays it as well
as C. P. Snow's *The Conscience of the Rich* reveals the closely
knit society of London's wealthy Jews. In some ways the Jews
and the Catholics are similar in the insularity of the lives they
lead in England. Both groups have a social structure apart from
that of either the Anglican or the nonconformist society, but
both Catholics and Jews are often participants in Protestant social life. The Irish-Catholics, however, are even more set apart
than the non-Irish Catholics like those seen in Evelyn Waugh's
novels. The Irish-Catholics are forced by religion and ethnic

background to create a social life for themselves that excludes most of their neighbors. Ironically, those who have money are even more restricted than the poor, for they are at home no-where. The Brandons, of *The Jealous God,* for instance, are not at home among the Dungarvans "because they had more money"; "and they wouldn't be at home among the Charbury business men because they were Catholics—and Irish to make it worse . . ." (180).

The whole pattern of life for the Dungarvans and their co-religionists is well developed. The social circle that revolves around the various church clubs, the inter-relationships between the Irish-Catholic families, the Hibernian Club that has a membership made up of Vincent's father's friends, the parochial school—all these things put Vincent's family and friends in a separate world. Using this social-religious circle as a microcosm, Braine paints us a universal (yet parochial) picture of life. The picture is universal in that man's sense of sin causes him anguish; parochial, because the particular practices of his church cause Vincent to define and realize his sin.

The whole tenor of the novel is governed by its social-religious background. For instance, the Hibernian Club, or the "Hibs," as its members call it, is Irish to the core—almost the English replica of a County Cork pub. Made up of "respectable and responsible Catholics, mainly middle class," the club is housed in a large, unfashionable Victorian mansion in a part of town once fashionable, but now the surrounding area is all "offices and consulting-rooms and showrooms." The solid professional men who built the district no longer live in Cord Street, which is destined to be razed soon. The club itself smells of "stone-dust and old plaster and half-rotten wood." The condition of the club is representative of the decayed social life and stifling separateness of the people who belong. The red plush curtain which cuts off the main room of the club from the street cannot be shut. Vincent, who is a traditionalist and a conservative, is irritated by the curtain, the state of the club, and the decline of the neighborhood: "In his father's time, he thought, there wouldn't have been any curtains that couldn't be drawn or any unsteady tables or worn carpeting or unpolished brass; the club was going downhill along with the neighborhood" (46). Vincent's attitude toward life is revealed in these musings: he longs for a simpler and more stable world of yesterday. His yearnings for Laura make him a rebel, and yet the staunch Irish-Catholic traditionalism that he displays in the scene where he inspects the Hibernian Club's curtain makes defection impossible.

Similar to club and church in influence is the tightly knit family circle that is central to the book. Braine makes the prying Dungarvan-Rosslea family a very real and maddening institution in *The Jealous God*. Nothing that Vincent does escapes the notice of some member of his clannish family, for some cousin or aunt always sends a message of his malefactions along the tribal telegraph. Although Paul's wife Jenny has known Laura in library school, Paul himself first hears of her from a friend; and later he learns of Vincent's interest in Laura from his brother and sister-in-law: "Matthew and Maureen say she's most delectable" (229). Immediately the word spreads among the family that she is a Protestant. Mrs. Dungarvan learns of Laura's existence from "other people": "Oh, they enjoyed telling me. 'Your son's got himself a girl, Mrs. Dungarvan'" (110). In summary, the whole Dungarvan network operates by hearsay and innuendo. Even the old grandmother, the most sensible and human member of the tribe, learns what everyone is doing through the agency of priests and relatives.

The family is militantly Catholic, even to the point of classifying the merest acquaintances by religion. Matthew announced to Vincent "I lunched with a Methodist" (40). And Paul disapproves of Vincent's newspaper because he remembers that "No Catholic can be an editor of the *Observer*." Vincent says he doesn't want to be an editor, and "Anyway they changed that" (91). Mrs. Dungarvan almost always refers to Laura as "that Protestant woman." The grandmother reads Evelyn Waugh and Graham Greene; she feels guilty about reading and liking John O'Hara—"He seems to have lost the grace of God, but he knows what men are like" (195).

The novel is flooded with descriptions of Irish, Catholic, and small-town Yorkshire family life; and the accuracy of the descriptions makes the novel come alive. The New York *Herald Tribune* reviewer praises the "unself-consciousness" of Braine's picture of local life and says, "The people he mimics do not see themselves as quaint or touching or amusing—and neither does Braine. They see themselves as the human norm, and so does Braine. His attitude is neutral as a window. And yet class, social conditioning is the most interesting character in the book. . . ." [5]

Another critic has called "the sense of the family group" the most successful aspect of the book, and he asserts that "The

reader gets the impression of life lived on every side, which, as
Henry James pointed out, is the chief function of the novel. . . ." [6]
Certainly, anyone who reads the book can see that the picture
of one facet of Yorkshire life is done very well indeed. In fact, I
think that *The Jealous God* is Braine's best handling of the
purely local life; moreover, he manages to use his milieu as a
framework on which to build the solid structure of a good novel.

IV *Style*

It is also evident in *The Jealous God* that Braine has learned
something new about style. The kind of writing that marked
Room and *Life at the Top* (and to a lesser degree *The Vodi*)
has been considerably modified in his fourth novel. Where
Braine's early style tended to short, choppy sentences and to
abrupt speech, *The Jealous God* is written in a more leisurely,
mature manner. The sentences are generally longer, and the dialogue seems the sort of language that people speak. One reason
for the changed style of the fourth novel is that the subject
matter is different, especially from that of the two Joe Lampton
novels. Where life was hard, polished, and chromium-plated in
the first and third books, it is much slower and more provincial
in *The Jealous God*. And one mark of maturity in a novelist is
his ability to make the style reflect the theme, plot, and characters
of the work. Joe Lampton's anxious attempt to climb atop the
Warley heap is clearly reflected in his brittle descriptions of
Yorkshire life. We should contrast the following typical description from *Room at the Top* with the style of *The Jealous God*:

The Aston-Martin started with a deep, healthy roar. As it passed
the cafe in the direction of St. Clair Road I noticed the young man's
olive linen shirt and bright silk neckerchief. The collar of the shirt
was tucked inside the jacket; he wore the rather theatrical ensemble
with a matter-of-fact nonchalance. Everything about him was easy and
loose but not tired or sloppy. He had an undistinguished face with a
narrow forehead and mousy hair cut short with no oil on it. It was a
rich man's face, smooth with assurance and good living. (29)

The following passage, selected almost at random from *The Jealous God* is, I think, typical of the natural descriptive prose style
that marks that novel. It is more reflective and less like an American detective story than some of Braine's early work. It is not
involuted and full of qualifications; it is less hurried and more
balanced, yet clean and hard:

He pulled down the window and took a deep breath; it was as if
he were assimilating the trees, the steep hillside sweeping up to the
moors, the undulating hills against the skyline, the grey tatters of
cloud over the new moon, the sense of winter coming and the sense
of remoteness, of departure from human concerns. Now that the
engine had stopped, he could hear the sounds of the woods, the faint
rustlings, the creaking of branches in the breeze, an owl hooting far
away, then nearer and louder and longer, and then what might have
been the scream of some small animal; there was violence here and
pain and terror but without fuss, it was as beautiful in its way as the
Roman encirclement of the Brigantes must have been. (34)

The handling of dialogue in the fourth novel also indicates an
advance over the other books. There are no embarrassing lapses
of speech such as those of the children in *Life at the Top*. In
The Jealous God everyone speaks in what seems to me to be
real, unaffected language. The following exchange between Vincent and his aged grandmother is quite ordinary but is like the
speech of the rest of the novel in that the speech patterns reflect
the class, education, and personality of the characters:

"Why did she divorce him?"
"We haven't talked about it very much. He was unfaithful to her.
That's all I know."
"There'd be more to it than that," his grandmother said. "From
what I've heard, she's a sensible girl. If every wife had to leave her
husband for that reason, there wouldn't be many that weren't divorced. Not that Protestants see things as we do, poor creatures."
"I sometimes wish I'd been one," he said. "I wouldn't have any
problems then, would I?"
"There's many a good Catholic wished that before you, child. It
won't help you to wish for what you can't have." (196)

Gone are Braine's attempts to burn with a gem-like flame; gone
is the Hemingway stichomythia that often edged its way into
the early books. Braine is more able to have all his characters
reflect themselves with their speech than he was in the first three
books. And this accomplishment accounts for the larger number
of good and believable characters in *The Jealous God*. It also
accounts for something that has not been mentioned before in
this chapter—Braine's decreasing use of brand names and consumer goods to fix a character in his social and geographical
milieu. We cannot say that the author eschews the names of
goods completely in his fourth novel, for it would be uncharac-
teristic of him never to mention a make of car or a cigarette

name. But he relies surprisingly little on this overworked but not ineffective device.

V *Critique*

In general, the novel, as I have tried to show, is good; and no admirer of Braine needs to apologize for it. *The Jealous God* is not, however, a great novel; the flaws are all too evident to a discerning reader. But its defects are far outweighed by its good qualities: the characters, style, and theme make up for the weakness of plot; the steady focus and serious intent make the reader willing to forget the contrived ending that saves Vincent.

Certainly, the novel marks a turning point in Braine's career. It shows clearly that the promise he showed in *Room at the Top* and in *The Vodi* did not die in the *Life at the Top* fiasco. He learned most of the lessons he needed to learn as a novelist somewhere between his first and fourth books. It is a shame that his best book so far has enjoyed less fame than *Life at the Top;* perhaps the lack of sensational issues in *The Jealous God* made it less discussed. However, this novel is likely to have a much longer life than Braine's other works, for not only is it better artistically, but it is less tied to transient events than *Room* and *Life at the Top*. Perceptive critics saw clearly that *The Jealous God* was Braine's most serious and most worthwhile book to date.

CHAPTER 7

Conclusion

SINCE 1957, when John Braine burst full-blown onto the literary scene, he has matured considerably. He has learned a great deal about handling character, his style has been refined, he has set himself the task of exploring more serious themes, and he has been successful (after some faltering) in handling point of view and focus. He still does not handle plot construction capably; but he has made some progress over the years.

I *Development of Characters*

His ability to depict character successfully was questioned by some of the reviewers, especially after the failure of *Life at the Top*. Joe Lampton in the first novel was a believable character, as was Alice Aisgill, though to a somewhat lesser extent; but the other characters in that novel were generally lifeless. Since Joe was the first-person narrator, the reader had a chance to see what he was thinking and to identify with him. But there was a tendency for Joe to delineate other characters in a clever phrase or to tie them to something they owned or wished to own. Joe made much of calling others Zombies—successful Zombies or working-class Zombies. He used the term to describe the people in Warley and Dufton who were so dehumanized as to be walking dead—and, ironically, the term might also have been applied justly to most of the characters in the book.

Except for its two major characters, who were not badly depicted, *The Vodi* shows limited growth in characterization techniques. The father of Dick Corvey, however, showed some signs of coming to life, and there were a number of good caricatures who fell little short of being rounded characters. There was still a tendency, though, to define and describe a character by what he owned or wore—this as a substitute for more mature analysis or objective dramatization.

Whatever life existed in Joe Lampton in the first novel was gone by the time of *Life at the Top*. Joe himself became one of the Zombies he talked about; and, when the reader loses any sense of identity with Joe, he finds it hard to care much about the people who surround him. Not only are the characters weak in the third novel; they seem to be so poorly motivated that any interest one might otherwise have is destroyed.

The Jealous God shows an astonishing advance over Life at the Top, for Braine learned how to make a character come alive without relying on brand names to give him individuality. He learned that successful characters in fiction develop from within and are not brilliantly spotlighted by a formulated phrase, that the brand of cigarettes a man smokes tells more about his tastes than about his inherent qualities. In addition to Vincent himself, other characters come to life: the mother, the grandmother, the girl Laura, and some very minor figures. Braine seems to have learned from his early novels what an author can do and what he must avoid in order to create life-like people. One thing he does better in The Jealous God is to allow the characters to speak and act more for themselves. Readers come to know characters by what they say, by what they do, and by what others (narrator, characters, the author) say about them. The first two approaches are artistically sounder; in The Jealous God Braine shows that he has learned that lesson. Here, he is not so impatient that he cannot wait for a character to reveal himself without the author's apparent help. An example is the old grandmother, who is only slowly revealed as the most broadminded and clear-sighted person in the novel. Her nature is not clear to the reader until late in the book, and the reader has a feeling of coming to know her as he does any real-life acquaintance.

II Narrative Techniques

Another thing that Braine has learned is the effective use of something other than first-person narration. Room and Life at the Top are both told in first-person, "I-as-major-character" narration, generally considered the easiest device for an author. In fact, a great many first novels are written in first person because their authors are incompetent to handle any other technique. Room at the Top was a successful example of the first-person narrative technique; for, while it was vital that the reader see and understand the motives of the man at the center of the action, it was not necessary to know the other characters in the book especially well. Having chosen first-person for Room at the Top, the author was almost committed to the same point of view in the sequel. It was either that or write a very different novel from the one he apparently intended. Braine had no chance to learn new narrative methods for *Life at the Top;* it was one of those books that teaches an author never to go back to characters and events already fully exploited.

Meanwhile, between the two Lampton novels, Braine had tried in *The Vodi* one of the most subtle points of view possible —third-person narration with a shifting focus. The reader is allowed first to see into the mind of Dick Corvey and then into the mind of Evelyn Mallaton. Perhaps the chief weakness of the shifting focus in *The Vodi* was that Braine permitted the scenes to change too rapidly, and the reader had barely fixed his attention on one character when a shift occurred. This criticism is especially true of the last half of the book; in the first part, when the focus is on Dick, the novel holds together better and is more sharply focused.

Some of the weakness of method in *The Vodi* results from the excessive use of flashbacks. Braine's choice of the flashback technique—like that of the shifting focus—was good; the execution, however, was faulty. The flashbacks were useful in revealing Dick Corvey's past and showing its influence on his present plight, but there was some difficulty in telling what part of his life he was remembering. Also, the time shifts collided with the person shifts, and before the reader could adjust himself to one character, one tone, or one time, another change occurred. The end of the book is made up of a dizzying series of switches.

The Jealous God avoids all the pitfalls of *The Vodi,* but not by going back to first-person narrative as Braine did in *Life at the Top.* The point of view of the fourth novel is third person, limited omniscience, with the focus steadily on Vincent Dungarvan. The effect gained by keeping the focus on the central character is similar to that of *Room at the Top,* except that the author makes Vincent come alive by dramatizing and objectifying his plight rather than by describing him directly to the reader. And the other characters are better seen when Braine is forced by the method of the novel to present them and make them act and react to Vincent. There is no easy dismissal of characters by the narrator in *The Jealous God,* for the narrator is hidden from view. Thus, like a dramatist, Braine must follow the advice of Henry James to make characters act out their problems. This novel is closer to drama than *Room at the Top,* which is confessional in tone and form.

III *Plot*

As we have already noted, plot is still a problem for John Braine, and in *The Jealous God* he is no more skillful than he was in his first novel. It is not that Braine cannot weave an interesting tale, for his stories usually hold the attention of the reader. But he is never able to construct his novels so that they work themselves out logically without the aid of the author. He resorts in at least three of them to a kind of modern *deus ex machina*. In *Room at the Top*, when Susan becomes pregnant, he must marry her (as he wanted to do); and Alice's fortuitous death removes her from Joe's and Susan's lives. In *Life at the Top*, Joe is saved from an intolerable situation by the illness of his little son, surely a most contrived and overused B-movie device for reuniting estranged couples. In *The Jealous God*, Braine resorts again to the expedient of authorial murder: Vincent's involvement and his misery can only be solved by the death of Laura's husband.

There are a number of cases in all four novels where the author's plot manipulations stand out crudely. Coincidence is used, as I have already pointed out, to entangle and then to disentangle the plots. Usually the most obvious manipulations occur in the endings, for Braine's usual practice is to let the story develop out of the nature of the characters until the climax of the action. Then—and this is especially true of *The Jealous God* —when the character is thoroughly trapped by his own nature, Braine "solves" his problems. I can offer no defense for Braine's heavy-handed rescues, for they certainly have a tendency to spoil the novels, especially if one sees plot as the chief organizing principle around which all other parts of a literary work are grouped. However, if one considers plot as only one of the aspects of fiction—equal to character, style, theme—the flaws in Braine's plots are slightly less disturbing.

IV *Style*

The style of Braine's writing has changed greatly over the eight years of his novelistic career. One stylistic trait that has remained constant, however, is his ability to write clearly and simply. The six early sketches prefigure the first novel in that they are simple to the point of being journalistic. This is not to say that Braine is deficient in the same way that some journalists are, that he is subliterate and addicted to primer sentences. But from the start he is clear and crisp in the same way that the young Hemingway was; the early sketches and *Room at the Top* are written in what I have described in another place as Americanized style. The sentences are short and hard-hitting; and, as in Hemingway's work, there are few qualifications and parentheses. There is little subordination in the terse and self-sustaining sentences. The same is true of the dialogue in the first novel, for the characters speak in the same short, succinct sentences. The following passage from *Room at the Top* is typical:

> I found myself crumpling up my freshly lit cigarette. I threw it away and lit another with a shaking hand. She kept on talking, her voice low and controlled. "Get this clear, I own my body. I'm not ashamed of it. I'm not ashamed of anything I've ever done. If you'd ever mix with intelligent people you'd not be looking at me now as if I'd committed a crime." She laughed. It was an ugly harsh laugh which made my hair prickle. (146)

The Hemingway-Dashiel Hammett-Raymond Chandler influence can be seen in the passage. In fact, the Hemingway style has had as much influence on English writing as on American. Anthony Powell, one of the best English novelists of the postwar period, has said that perhaps the greatest influence on British writing after 1925 was Hemingway—"When I read *The Sun Also Rises,* for example, what I noticed was the dialogue, the way he got rid of all the excess verbiage. . . ." [1] Powell's own style, like that of many other British writers, grew away from being imitative of Hemingway; yet the influence remains to a considerable extent, especially in the writing of the working-class and lower-middle-class writers.

While *The Vodi* has a more sophisticated point of view than *Room at the Top,* it has a much less sharply defined style, as befits the theme. The slower, less sophisticated life depicted in the second novel does not require the taut style of *Room at the Top,* and the simpler provincial world is reflected in the relaxed style of the book. The dialogue is less staccato, and the narrative style is not so fast paced.

Life at the Top is in all respects such an imitation of his first novel that Braine attempts to recapture the pace of the action and the style of *Room at the Top.* But, as I have indicated, the style and pace—indeed the whole book—is a pallid imitation. The appropriately spare style for a tight and bitter story about an interloper among the rich cannot be sustained in describing Joe's disintegration after he has joined them. As a result, the style is as flabby as the man.

The Jealous God is a turning point for Braine in a number of ways, not the least of which is the growth of a mature style. The writing in his first two novels is appropriate for the material but it is not definitely and uniquely Braine's own. The style of *The Jealous God* is. And he is comfortable when using it. The sentences are longer and the dialogue is less curt, but there is no sacrifice of readability. The ability to shape the characters of this novel is partly a result of the improvement in dialogue style. In some of the earlier works, the talk was so monosyllabic that the characters came through only as crude, partly realized figures. With the flexibility of the dialogue in *The Jealous God*, the characters seem more real. Braine lets them have their say in an unself-conscious manner, and the reader is able to apprehend them more fully than the often tongue-tied persons of the first three novels.

None of these comments ought to suggest that Braine is a preeminent stylist. He is not. At best it can be said that his style is clear and pleasant, and, in the fourth novel at least, well adapted to theme, character, and plot. At its worst, his style is somewhat journalistic in the sense of possessing readability but lacking solidity. When he is good, he is swift-moving, clear and readable; when he is bad, he is slick and overly facile.

V *Theme*

The themes that Braine has treated are all serious and important. The first novel explored the problems that a man bent on success in life has to face in making his mark on the world. *Room at the Top* shows how it feels for a man to barter away his soul in attempting to find a place in the affluent society that began to exist for the lower middle classes in the British provinces after World War II. In *Life at the Top*, a theme is treated which is very much akin to the one in the first novel—what it is like when one has sold himself and realizes that the life he won is cheap and trivial. Both these novels treat themes that are fundamental in modern society; the defects in the two books do not stem from a triviality of theme.

But there is, as I have said elsewhere, some confusion about Braine's attitude toward Joe in both *Room* and *Life at the Top*. He seems to sympathize with Joe at times when no sympathy is required; that is, he seems to feel that the pressures of the age made it impossible for Joe to do otherwise. That is clearly not the case. Joe makes his decision to sell his soul for wealth; not everyone does. And those who do not find it hard to have an excess of sympathy for Joe Lampton, especially in view of the fact that Joe gets everything he wants except, of course, peace of mind. If one is wholly intent on money and is willing to sacrifice himself for it, the money should be all that it is necessary for us to grant him. Braine seems to me to be equivocal in his own mind about how much sorrow we need feel for Joe.

The lonely and enervating nature of failure is the theme of *The Vodi,* and again Braine chooses a worthwhile subject for his novel but lets his own feelings about things confuse the reader. The Vodi, the gnomelike creatures that Dick Corvey blames for his misfortune, seem at first to have some bearing on the main character's misfortune. They seem to be furies whose evil relieves Dick of responsibility, but then we learn that Dick Corvey is responsible for all that has happened to him. Only when that becomes clear can the reader see the point of the theme and put the novel into perspective. Also, the themes of the first three novels are concerned with responsibility for one's decisions and deeds. Dick and Joe must accept responsibility, but Braine is remiss in his treatment of the themes because he has an ambivalent and unclear attitude toward personal responsibility. By the end of *The Vodi* we are satisfied that Dick is to blame; we then ask why Braine let us be as fooled by the Vodi as Dick was in the first of the novel. There are no satisfactory answers to these questions.

Putting aside the problem of success, *The Jealous God* studies the moral struggle of the Catholic who falls in love with a divorced person. In addition to the purely sectarian problem, there is again inherent in the theme questions about the responsibility that a man must take for his decisions and actions. The matter of Vincent's Catholicism provides the framework for the larger question that seems to me to be at the heart of the book—how much one's conscience causes him to pay for his desires. I do not feel that Braine is a Catholic novelist in the usual sense of that term. Although he is a Catholic, he is more concerned with Vincent as a man run afoul of his conscience than with problems of dogma. Even in a novel by John Braine, Vincent could have endured his problems in some other context—Joe Lampton does. Catholicism simply provides a very good framework for the torture and harassment that Vincent suffers.

The themes explored in the four novels show that Braine's view of the world is not altogether pleasant. He himself said in an interview that he is not an especially happy man—"Happiness does not seem all that significant to me."[2] He is greatly concerned with the harshness of life, with people who make wrong or wicked decisions, with people who have to live with their sin and guilt and loneliness. Richard Hoggart, reviewing *Life at the Top*, pointed out that pessimism and anxiety are predominant themes in Braine's novels—there is an attitude that the "world is horrible" and "everyone gets hurt." There are also loneliness, guilt, self-distrust, and a desire for self-justification on the part of several characters. The loneliness, Hoggart says, can be seen in the searches for a mature woman to be wife and mother and the camaraderie with servants and "others who can't make serious emotional demands."[3]

It seems not wide of the mark to say that Braine has a strong sense of original sin as well as a definite feeling that the modern world and its weakened moral and religious values are responsible for man's unhappy state. There is always the hint in the novels that some time in the past was more desirable—the uncomplicated life of Joe's parents in Dufton; the pre-war childhood of Dick; the early days of the Dungarvan clan in Yorkshire. Even the six sketches picture an idyllic past—"Irish Quarter" tells of happier times before Pakistanis and other poor people moved to Silsbridge Lane. Braine seems to be saying that man's innate evil keeps changing things for the worse.

An Irish-Catholic upbringing in Protestant Yorkshire and serious attacks of tuberculosis some years ago have, no doubt, helped to shape Braine's outlook. His religious training certainly must have stressed original sin, and the illnesses must have confirmed his belief that everyone is likely to get hurt and suffer loneliness and anxiety. But if his life has made him pessimistic, it has also made him tolerant of human weakness. One of the things that makes Braine's novels interesting is his willingness to treat weak characters sympathetically, for one theme that runs throughout all the novels concerns the person who suffers because of his human weakness. And far from being an angry writer, Braine tends to be a very sympathetic and old-fashioned novelist who holds onto belief in God and in the recoverability of man.

VI *Critique*

Braine, on the basis of the novels he has written, is not a major British novelist. There is no question that he has talent, and it seems to me that his most recent novel shows a maturity that was not evident in the three that he wrote earlier. The impact of *Room at the Top* on the reading public was great—greater perhaps than the merit of the novel should have justified. And that success caused readers and reviewers to expect more of him than he was immediately able to produce.

The second novel, while it showed courage in deserting the Joe Lampton theme, was not a success; and the third returned unsatisfactorily to Joe Lampton. Its lack of success, however, did not keep Braine from writing a strong fourth novel on a theme hitherto untried by him. In *The Jealous God* he found a kind of novel that should prove to be his most suitable medium —the novel that centers around the actual life of lower-middle-class provincial families. It is true that novels about Irish-Catholic provincial life do not have the sensational glamor and reader appeal that the shiny picture of Warley society has. But the success of *Room at the Top*, at least for judicious readers, lay not so much in showing how the wealthy lived and thought as in how a hungering small-town boy from the North saw them. The best thing about *The Vodi* and *The Jealous God* was the total reality of the sense of place. If Braine will confine himself to the Yorkshire he knows and leave the society novel to others, he will almost certainly be more lastingly successful than he has been.

Personally, I hope that Braine will continue his present tack and write more fully about the life that he knows well and that has been little explored in recent British fiction. Sociologically, the North Country has undergone more change since World War II than has London, the locale of most Establishment novels. Americanization, the rise of the Joe Lampton élite, and the spread of public education have vastly changed life in the provinces. Even the picture of small-town life in William Cooper's *Scenes From Provincial Life,* which was set before the war, is not much like Braine's. Braine can do a service by rendering that life as accurately as he has done in *The Vodi* and in *The Jealous God.*

If he does continue his provincial studies, perhaps he will receive better critical treatment than in the past. Serious criticism of his works is almost non-existent, though all his novels have been reviewed widely and intelligently in the British and American quality weeklies and monthlies. In the four chapters devoted to Braine's novels, I have summarized or mentioned most of the significant reviews. These are generally adequate, but they do not give a real insight into Braine's fiction. The two reviews by Richard Hoggart mentioned in this study are, I think, the soundest and most perceptive. There are few scholarly studies of his work in American academic quarterlies, and those that exist are rudimentary. William Van O'Connor's essay, "Two Types of 'Heroes' in Post-War British Fiction," [4] is short and not so much concerned with Braine as with a type of hero represented by Joe Lampton. The essay by John Hurrell in *Critique* called "Class and Conscience in John Braine and Kingsley Amis," [5] is mostly about Kingsley Amis and devotes only a page or two to Braine.

G. S. Frazer gives about two pages to Braine in *The Modern Writer and his World* and F. R. Karl about the same space in *A Reader's Guide to the Contemporary English Novel*, while the best treatment in a book is in Kenneth Allsop's *The Angry Decade*. Allsop, writing in 1958 before anything but *Room at the Top* had been published, devoted five pages to an intelligent discussion of the novel as well as to some biographical material. He sees the strengths as well as the weaknesses of the first novel and is generally sympathetic toward Braine.

To say again briefly what I have perhaps said too often, Braine is a good, solid writer who is just now coming to maturity as a novelist. He is relatively strong as a stylist and is learning to develop his characters adequately. His plots are not adequate because he is unable to let things proceed as naturally as they do in life; likewise his themes, though important, are often flawed by his ambivalent attitudes toward his material. His pictures of provincial England are the strongest points in the novels he has written so far, for he is always able to make locale a vital element. And he can relate the characters to their setting very effectively.

With his considerable talent, his tolerance of human weakness, and his total commitment to writing, Braine has the power to become a major figure in modern English fiction. It seems, with his fourth novel, that he has found himself as a novelist. If so, and if he is able to overcome some of the deficiencies that I have discussed, he will merit even more serious consideration in the future.

Notes and References

Chapter One

1. David Storey, "Journey Through a Tunnel," *Writers on Themselves*, ed. Herbert Read (London, 1964), p. 97.
2. *Ibid.*
3. *Ibid.*
4. John Braine, "Lunch with J. B. Priestley: Two Gentlemen from Bradford," *Encounter*, X (June, 1958), 8-14.
5. *Ibid.*, p. 9.
6. John Braine, "The Fog Lifts: John Bull's Schooldays," *Spectator*, CCI (August 18, 1958), 188-89.
7. *Ibid.*, p. 188.
8. Braine, "Lunch with J. B. Priestley," p. 12.
9. John Braine, "Image of the North," *The Listener*, LXIX (May 2, 1963), 749-50. Reprinted in *Town and Country Planning*, XXXI (June, 1963), 259-62.
10. *Ibid.*, pp. 749-50.
11. Kenneth Allsop, *The Angry Decade* (New York, 1958). This chapter owes a large debt to the concise and accurate discussion of the fiction of the 1950's that is found in Allsop's book.
12. G. S. Frazer, *The Modern Writer and His World* (London, 1964), p. 147.
13. Richard Hoggart, *The Uses of Literacy* (Boston, 1961). Hoggart's book was first published in London by Chatto and Windus, Ltd. in 1957.
14. Allsop, *The Angry Decade*, p. 43.
15. Leslie Paul, *Angry Young Man* (London, 1951).
16. John Osborne, "They Call it Cricket," *Declaration*, ed. Tom Maschler (New York, 1958).
17. Tom Maschler, "Introduction," in *Ibid.*, p. 8.
18. Osborne, "They Call it Cricket," p. 58.
19. *Ibid.*, p. 56.
20. *Ibid.*, p. 62.
21. Allsop, *The Angry Decade*, p. 103.
22. *Ibid.*, p. 98.
23. John Wain, *Sprightly Running* (London, 1963), p. 166.

118

24. *Living in the Present* (New York, 1960), p. 249.
25. *Ibid.*, p. v.
26. *Ibid.*, p. 85.
27. Robert Weaver, "England's Angry Young Men," *Queen's Quarterly*, LXV (Summer, 1958), 188.
28. James Gindin, *Post-War British Fiction* (Berkeley, 1962), p. 137.
29. Richard Hoggart, "Plain Man of Letters," *Nation*, CLXXXV (October 26, 1957), 285.
30. *Declaration*, p. 78.
31. *Ibid.*
32. *Ibid.*, p. 88.
33. Allsop, *The Angry Decade*, p. 68.
34. Colin Wilson, *The Outsider* (Boston, 1956), p. 15.
35. Allsop, *The Angry Decade*, pp. 148-82.
36. Arthur Schlesinger, Jr., *A Thousand Days: John F. Kennedy in the White House* (Boston, 1965), pp. 113-14.
37. *Ibid.*
38. Stuart Holroyd, *Emergence From Chaos* (London, 1957), Introduction.
39. Allsop, *The Angry Decade*, p. 73.
40. *Ibid.*

Chapter Two

1. "Something for Everyone," *The New Statesman*, XL (July 15, 1950), 65.
2. "Irish Quarter," *The New Statesman*, XLII (August 4, 1951), 124-25.
3. "Nowhere," *The New Statesman*, XLII (September 8, 1951), 250, 252.
4. "Number Nine Rock," *The New Statesman*, XLIII (March 29, 1952), 370-71.
5. *The New Statesman*, XLIII (April 19, 1952), 465.
6. "A Devil for Dancing," *The New Statesman*, XLVI (August 8, 1953), 153-54.
7. "Portrait of a Provincial Intellectual," *The New Statesman*, LIV (October 5, 1957), 421-22.

Chapter Three

1. *Times Literary Supplement* (April 5, 1957), p. 205.
2. John Davenport, *The Observer* (March 17, 1957), p. 14.
3. Charles Rolo, *The Atlantic*, CC (November, 1957), 247.
4. Alan Herrington, *The Nation*, CLXXXV (December 7, 1957), 438.
5. Philip Deasy, *Commonweal*, LXVII (December 7, 1957), 340.

6. Whitney Balliett, *The New Yorker,* XXXIII (November 2, 1957), 186-89.

7. James Stern, New York *Times Book Review* (October 13, 1957), pp. 5, 36.

8. Kenneth Allsop, *The Angry Decade* (London, 1958), p. 82.

9. *Room at the Top,* pp. 23-24. This and subsequent references are to the first American edition (Boston, 1958).

10. Sir Richard Rees, *George Orwell: Fugitive from the Camp of Victory* (Carbondale, 1962), p. 15.

11. Deasy, *Commonweal,* p. 340.

12. James Gray, *Saturday Review,* XL (October 19, 1957), 20.

13. *Ibid.*

14. Stern, New York *Times Book Review,* p. 36.

15. Allsop, *The Angry Decade,* p. 82.

16. G. S. Frazer, *The New Statesman,* LIII (March 16, 1957), 358.

17. Balliett, *The New Yorker,* p. 188.

18. James Gindin, *Post-War British Fiction* (Berkeley, 1962), p. 108.

19. The influence of Raymond Chandler has also been noted by G. S. Frazer in *The Modern Writer and His World,* p. 181.

20. *Ibid.*

21. Harry Hopkins, *The New Look* (London, 1963), p. 353.

22. Frazer, *The Modern Writer and His World,* p. 181.

23. Deasy, *Commonweal,* p. 340.

Chapter Four

1. Gabriel Pearson, *The New Statesman,* LVIII (November 21, 1959), 718.

2. *From the Hand of the Hunter.* This and subsequent references are to the first American edition (Boston, 1960).

3. Martin Price, *Yale Review,* LXIX (March, 1960), 445.

4. Pearson, *The New Statesman,* p. 718.

5. *Time,* LXXV (April 4, 1960), p. 98.

6. *Ibid.*

7. Pearson, *The New Statesman,* p. 718.

8. *Ibid.*

9. Price, *Yale Review,* p. 445.

10. Richard Hoggart, *Manchester Guardian* (November 20, 1959), p. 8.

11. *Ibid.*

12. *Ibid.*

Chapter Five

1. Robert Gutwillig, "A Talk in London with John Braine," New York *Times Book Review* (October 7, 1962), p. 5.
2. *Life at the Top*, p. 3. This and subsequent references are to the first American edition (Boston, 1962).
3. Granville Hicks, *Saturday Review*, XLV (October 6, 1962), 21.
4. Richard Hoggart, *Manchester Guardian Weekly* (October 5, 1962), p. 11.
5. E. M. Forster, *Aspects of the Novel* (New York, 1956), p. 78.
6. *Ibid.*, p. 73.
7. *Times Literary Supplement* (October 5, 1962), p. 773.
8. Milton Rugoff, New York *Herald Tribune Books* (September 30, 1962), p. 4.
9. *Times Literary Supplement*, p. 773.
10. A. Alvarez, *The New Statesman*, LXIV (October 5, 1962), 458.
11. *Ibid.*
12. *Times Literary Supplement*, p. 773.
13. Walter Allen, New York *Times Book Review* (October 7, 1962), p. 5.
14. Hilary Corke, *New Republic*, CXLVII (November 3, 1962), 24.
15. *Ibid.*
16. Alvarez, *The New Statesman*, p. 458.
17. *Time* (December 17, 1965), p. 101.
18. Alvarez, *The New Statesman*, p. 458.
19. Hicks, *Saturday Review*, p. 21.
20. Alvarez, *The New Statesman*, p. 458.
21. Hoggart, *Manchester Guardian Weekly*, p. 11.
22. Martin Price, *Yale Review*, LII (December, 1962), 265.
23. Mordecai Richler, *Spectator*, CCIX (October 19, 1962), 602.
24. *Times Literary Supplement*, p. 773.
25. Rugoff, New York *Herald Tribune Books*, p. 4.

Chapter Six

1. Peter Buitenhuis, New York *Times Book Review* (March 7, 1965), p. 4.
2. Wilfred Sheed, New York *Herald Tribune* (March 21, 1965), p. 4.
3. Granville Hicks, *Saturday Review* (March 6, 1965), p. 23.
4. *The Jealous God*, p. 287. This and all subsequent references are to the first American edition (Boston, 1965).
5. Sheed, New York *Herald Tribune Books*, p. 4.
6. Buitenhuis, New York *Times Book Review*, p. 4.

Chapter Seven

1. Donald M. Davis, "An Interview with Anthony Powell," *College English*, XXIV (April, 1963), 534-35.

2. Robert Gutwillig, "A Talk in London with John Braine," New York *Times Book Review* (October 7, 1962), p. 5.

3. Richard Hoggart, *Manchester Guardian Weekly*, p. 11.

4. William Van O'Connor, "Two Types of 'Heroes' in Post-War British Fiction," *PMLA*, LXXVII (March, 1962), 168-74.

5. John Hurrell, "Class and Conscience in John Braine and Kingsley Amis," *Critique*, II (Spring-Summer, 1958), 39-53.

Selected Bibliography

Primary Sources

1. Novels

Room at the Top. London: Eyre and Spottiswood, 1957. Boston: Houghton Mifflin Co., 1957.

The Vodi. London: Eyre and Spottiswood, 1959. Published in America as *From the Hand of the Hunter.* Boston: Houghton Mifflin Co., 1960.

Life at the Top. London: Eyre and Spottiswood, 1962. Boston: Houghton Mifflin Co., 1962.

The Jealous God. London: Eyre and Spottiswood, 1964. Boston: Houghton Mifflin Co., 1965.

2. Short Pieces

"A Devil for Dancing." *The New Statesman,* XLVI (August 8, 1953), 153-54. Fictional sketch.

"Fog Lifts: John Bull's Schooldays." *Spectator,* CCI (August 8, 1958), 188-89. Autobiographical essay.

"From Bradford to Corfu." *The Listener,* XLIX (February 14, 1953), 279. Autobiographical essay.

"The Image of the North." *The Listener,* LXIX (May 2, 1963), 749-50. Reprinted in *Town and Country Planning,* XXXI (June, 1963), 259-62. Autobiographical essay.

"Irish Quarter." *The New Statesman,* XLII (August 4, 1951), 124-25. Fictional sketch.

"Lunch with J. B. Priestley: Two Gentlemen from Bradford." *Encounter,* X (June, 1958), 8-14. Interview.

"The Month, Personal Notes." *Twentieth Century,* LXIII (February, 1958), 168-75. Autobiographical essay.

"Nowhere." *The New Statesman,* XLII (September 8, 1951), 250. Fictional sketch.

"Number Nine Rock." *The New Statesman,* XLIII (March 29, 1952), 370-71. Fictional sketch.

"On Being a Public Librarian." *The Listener,* LXVI (December 14, 1961), 1022. Autobiographical essay.

"Portrait of a Provincial Intellectual." *The New Statesman,* LIV
(October 5, 1957), 421-22. Fictional sketch.
"Something for Everyone." *The New Statesman,* XL (July 11, 1950),
65. Fictional sketch.

Secondary Sources

The criticism of Braine's work is limited almost wholly to transitory
reviews of the novels; therefore, only a few scholarly and critical
articles devoted to him are listed in the secondary sources.

ALLSOP, KENNETH. *The Angry Decade.* New York: British Book
Centre, 1958. Pp. 78-85. Only *Room at the Top* had been written
when this study was published. It is a thoughtful discussion of
the novel and the social forces that helped shape it.

FRAZER, G. S. *The Modern Writer and His World.* Baltimore: Pen-
guin Books, 1964. Pp. 179-82. Short, negative review of *Room*
and *Life at the Top.* Calls style "whorish *chic,*" and says that
much of the social truth is "exposed unconsciously."

HURRELL, JOHN D. "Class and Conscience in John Braine and Kingsley
Amis." *Critique,* II (Spring-Summer, 1958), 39-53. Mainly a dis-
cussion of Amis, with brief mention of Braine and *Room at the
Top.*

KARL, FREDERICK R. "The Angries: Is There a Protestant in the
House?" *A Reader's Guide to the Contemporary English Novel.*
New York: Farrar, Straus and Cudahy, 1962. Pp. 229-31. Considers Braine as one of the "Angries." Talks only about *The Vodi*
and *Room at the Top.*

O'CONNOR, WILLIAM VAN. "Two Types of 'Heroes' in Post-War British
Fiction." *Publications of the Modern Language Association,*
LXXVII (March, 1962), 168-74. Short general discussions of a
number of "heroes" of modern fiction—those of Storey, Amis,
Waterhouse, Sillitoe, Hinde, Enright, Wain, Larkin. Two or three
paragraphs devoted to *Room at the Top* and Joe Lampton.

TAYLOR, ARCHER. "John Braine's Proverbs." *Western Folklore,* XXIII
(January, 1964), 42-43. Catalogs and discusses the proverbs
found in Braine's novels. Makes no literary judgments.

Index

Allen, Walter, 90
Allsop, Kenneth, *The Angry Decade*, 18, 30, 31, 33, 53, 117
Alvarez, A., 94
Amis, Kingsley, 19, 20, 21-24, 33, 34, 38, 40, 52, 57, 117; *Lucky Jim*, 20, 21-22, 23, 24, 27, 35, 37; *Take a Girl Like You*, 23; *That Uncertain Feeling*, 23
"Angry Young Men," 18-19, 24, 25, 27, 38, 57, 58, 62
Anouilh, Jean, 50
The Atlantic, 52

Balliett, Whitney, 52
Braine, John, life, 13, 15-18; parents, 13; education, 16
WRITINGS OF:
"A Devil for Dancing," 49-50
"Irish Quarter," 15, 45-46, 48, 49, 115
The Jealous God, 15, 17-18, 45-46, 48, 51, *95-107*, 109, 110, 111, 113, 114, 116
Life at the Top, 14, 15, 17, 26, 46, 51, 62, *82-94*, 95, 105, 106, 107, 108, 109, 110, 111, 112, 113, 115
"Life at the Top" (motion picture), 17
"Nowhere," 46-47
"Number Nine Rock," 48-49
"Portrait of a Provincial Intellectual," 50-51
Room at the Top, 13, 14, 15, 17, 20, 22, 26, 33, 37, 43, 46, 47, 48, 50, *52-68*, 70, 72, 77, 78, 79, 82, 84, 86, 87, 88, 89, 90, 92, 93, 94, 95, 102, 105, 107, 109, 110, 111, 112, 113, 116, 117

"Room at the Top" (motion picture), 13
"Something for Everyone," 43-44
The Vodi (From the Hand of the Hunter), 15, 17, 49, *69-81*, 86, 88, 89, 92, 93, 95, 97, 102, 105, 107, 108, 110, 112, 114, 116
Buitenhuis, Peter, 95

Camus, Albert, 30
Cary, Joyce, 19
Chandler, Raymond, 65, 112
Commonweal, 52, 56, 67
Cooper, William, 20-21, 29, 116; *Scenes From Married Life*, 20; *Scenes From Provincial Life*, 20, 116; *The Young People*, 20-21
Corvey, Dick, 15, *69-81*, 100, 108, 110, 114, 115
Coward, Noel, 24, 50
Critique, 117

The Daily Express, 13, 53, 91, 92
Declaration (ed. by Tom Maschler), 25-26, 29-30, 38
Dostoyevsky, Fyodor, 30
Dreiser, Theodore, *An American Tragedy*, 52
Dungarvan, Vincent, 15, *95-107*, 109, 110, 111, 114, 115

Eliot, T. S., 14, 19, 32

Fitzgerald, F. Scott, 53
Forster, E. M., 77, 86, 98
Frazer, G. S., 60; *The Modern Writer and His World*, 66, 67, 117
Fry, Christopher, 50

125